From Image
to Stitch

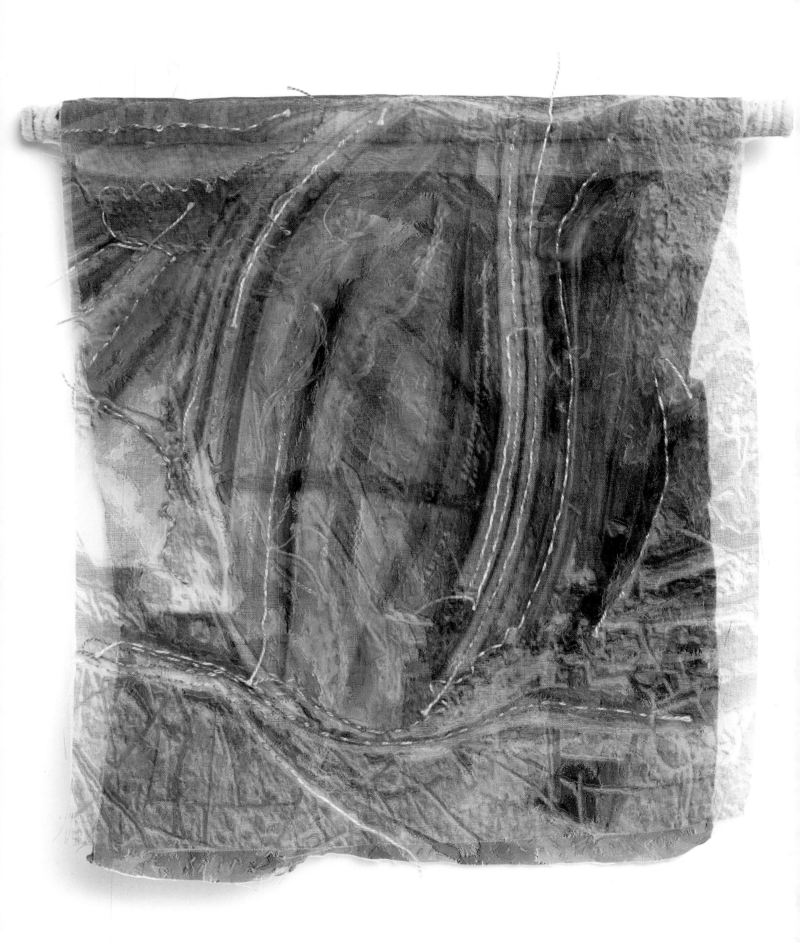

From Image to Stitch

Maggie Grey

BATSFORD

Acknowledgements

Grateful thanks to all my friends and colleagues who allowed me to include their work and to Michael Wicks for the photos. They have all made this a much better book.

This book is dedicated to Val Campbell-Harding – still my greatest inspiration.

More information can be found at www.imagetostitch.com

First published in the United Kingdom in 2008 by
Batsford
10 Southcombe Street
London W14 0RA

An imprint of Anova Books Company Ltd

ISBN: 978 19063 8802 7

A CIP catalogue record for this book is available from the British Library.

16 15 14 13 12 10 09 08
10 9 8 7 6 5 4 3 2 1

Reproduction by Rival Colour Ltd, UK
Printed by Craft Print Ltd, Singapore

This book can be ordered direct from the publisher at the website www.anovabooks.com, or try your local bookshop

Page 2: A small embroidery using identical prints on organza and cotton. The cotton base was hand embroidered using a variety of stitches, and was then wired to allow movement. Further delicate running stitches added interest to the sheer top layer, which was printed on ExtravOrganza. A piece of wrapped dowelling at the top keeps the two layers apart. Glynda Morrison.

Contents

Introduction

This book is about taking an image, whether a drawing, painting, digital photograph, computer design or photocopy, and using simple methods to turn it into a piece of textile art. The book assumes a minimum of technical knowledge, preferring a swift, hands-on approach. However, more detailed information is supplied in two appendices.

Ideas are given for those in search of inspiration and you are taken through a variety of techniques for creating the images. These range from producing a mixed-media artwork and scanning it, to using digital photographs or imaging software to create exciting effects.

It is perfectly possible to transfer an image to fabric using just tissue paper and Bondaweb (fusible webbing). However, the book progresses through a variety of other methods, such as the use of ordinary printer paper and unusual ways of building up fabrics for iron-over transfer techniques. We will be using materials that are easily obtainable and, other than an inkjet printer, very little is required in the way of special equipment. The materials used are shown and discussed in each chapter.

The heart of the book lies in the use of stitch. Having produced the image and transferred it to fabric, the next step is to enhance it with hand or machine embroidery. Innovative methods, both in the transfer and the stitch, are simplified and broken down into easy stages. From books to bangles, panels, bags and vessels, you will find lots of ideas here and the Conclusion (page 112) covers ways of building larger images to overcome the limitations of the inkjet printer.

Materials and equipment

You will probably be familiar with most of the materials used in this book, though others may be new to you. Some are very simple – what could be easier to find than tissue paper? A few are very specialized, such as an inkjet version of Shrink Plastic – what fun! In all cases, the 'Useful Stuff' section on pages 126–127 will tell you where to find them. Equipment comes down to a means of transferring information, a scanner or camera, a computer to receive it and an inkjet printer. If you have an all-in-one scanner, copier and printer, you can bypass the computer and print from the camera or photocopy your page. I think the printout is better from a computer, if possible. Most inkjet printers give very good results. If you want to be technical, check Appendix 2 on getting the best from your printer. None of the transfer methods suggested here should cause problems for the printer but I keep a very old printer and use it for experiments of an especially chunky nature.

Opposite: *Jazz Dance*
67 x 41 cm (26 x 16 inches)
This lively evocation of moving figures uses a heat-transferred digital print ironed onto cotton and dupion silk. This formed a base which was enhanced using reverse appliqué and hand-stitching techniques.
Olga Norris.

Below: Detail showing hand stitching.

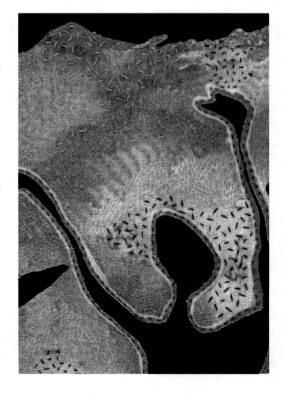

Inspiration and Images

There are many ways of finding inspiration and turning it into images that can be used as a basis for the ideas in this book. A sketchbook, even if it is only used for very rough sketches, can be an invaluable aid. You don't have to be an artist – think what can be done with tracing paper. Simple paper and paint techniques can also generate exciting images to be scanned. Digital cameras are accessible to most people and can be used very creatively to produce an image that can be used immediately.

Gathering information

When an idea strikes, it's time for the fun to begin. I prefer to produce work based on a theme, but one-offs are perfectly acceptable. The first step is to bring together all the information available on your chosen subject. Store it in a box file or folder. Use all the methods open to you. The Internet can be a good starting point – try using a search engine, as many of them have image libraries. It may not be possible to use downloaded pictures directly – check the copyright restrictions – but they can be printed out and used for reference.

Copyright-free books and CD-ROMs, such as the Dover or Search Press series, are invaluable. The local library can also be a rich source of inspirational material. Museum visits can really fire you up, and many allow photos to be taken.

Taking a sketchbook is a good idea. If you draw quickly and don't aim for perfection, a lively drawing will emerge. Make notes alongside, recording details of colour and shape. There are some excellent books on making and using sketchbooks, so check those listed in 'Useful Stuff'.

Previous page: *Chaos and Calm* 30 x 90 cm (12 x 36 inches) Pauline Parker was one of the selected artists for the Charles Henry Foyle Trust award. The subject given was the word 'maelstrom' and this piece was Pauline's response. Designs from her accompanying art book were manipulated in a paint program and printed onto fabric. They were then incorporated into a three-dimensional piece with added layers of dyed felt and free-machine embroidery, some on water-soluble fabric. Wire and copper tubing were used as a structural support.

Below left: A combination of the author's sketchbooks and a series of design boards by Valerie Campbell-Harding, based on egg-and-dart border patterns, shows how information can be gathered and displayed.

Below: Museum sketches, based on Islamic tiles and the motifs on Islamic pottery. Quick sketches and notes are helpful back-ups for photographs and concentrate the mind on searching for likely subjects for textile design.

Exploring a theme

When you've collected your material, consider how to consolidate it. Making a book is a good idea as, by building up the pages, you will be taking lots of the design decisions without getting too hung up on them. It can also suggest further directions for the textiles. Books can be hand made but a good strong sketchbook is fine. Make sure that the paper is strong enough to support a mix of paint, glue and collage. Paint and tracing methods are covered in depth throughout this book. They can all be used to build up the research materials and will suggest ways of extending the drawings and photos.

Design boards are an alternative to a book and carefully selected pieces of work can be displayed. Leading from an initial sketch to a finished piece, these can truly be called story boards.

Above: *Chaos and Calm* book.
This attractive book holds the artwork for the textile on page 8 and shows how ideas for the subject were explored. A personal slant was given to the interpretation of the word 'chaos', as Pauline related it to the regulation of her medical condition and the fact that ampoules of medication reverse her personal 'maelstrom' of chaotic breathing problems. She has incorporated the shape of the ampoules into her work.
Pauline Parker.

Using a camera

Regardless of the method of transfer, one of the best ways of recording images for your theme is by means of a camera, particularly if you have a digital camera. Museums will often allow photography if no flash is used but this can result in rather dark images. These can be retrieved to some extent by means of the Levels command – usually found under the 'Brightness and Contrast' section of the imaging or paint program's colour menus.

There are lots of ideas for improving your photographs on page 121.

Your image-upload computer program will probably have some special effects and these, used wisely, can add another dimension to your work. A good free program is called Picasa – see the 'Useful Stuff' section, pages 126–127, for more information.

Further ideas for using the camera will be described in detail as you work through the book.

Scanning your own designs

In this book you will find 'recipes' for mixed-media paper designs that can be scanned into your computer or photocopied onto transfer paper. This method of producing your own ready-to-stitch fabric is surprisingly quick and can be very satisfying. Scanners are very quick and easy to use but for a more detailed explanation, have a look at Appendix 1, which covers scanners.

Above: You can see from this screenshot that the 'Levels' option in Photoshop Elements can rescue dark and gloomy photographs.

Right: Consider the composition of a photograph before snapping away. This digital photograph of a Strelitzia plant involved getting in close to fill the screen with the main floral elements. The shapes work well and place the larger flower in a good position. This image could be printed out on fabric and would work well for many stitch techniques.

Right: In this photograph the image above has been manipulated using one of the special effects in a paint program. The colours have been changed using the Negative option, usually found in the Colour or Adjust menu.

Right: Finally a distortion, called Polar Co-ordinates, has been used on the resulting image to swirl it into interesting shapes. The floral source is still evident. One effect can be a little obvious but two can really give an exciting result.

Section 1
Print on Paper

The inks that we use in our inkjet printers today are much less likely to fade than they once were, so there is a lot you can do with printer papers. There are also products that can be used to enhance the print and improve the lightfast qualities. Paper is increasingly popular with textile artists and combines well with stitch. In this section, we consider using a variety, ranging from ordinary printer paper, tissue and brown paper to specialist papers for interesting effects. Mixed-media materials such as gesso and gels can be added, before or after stitching.

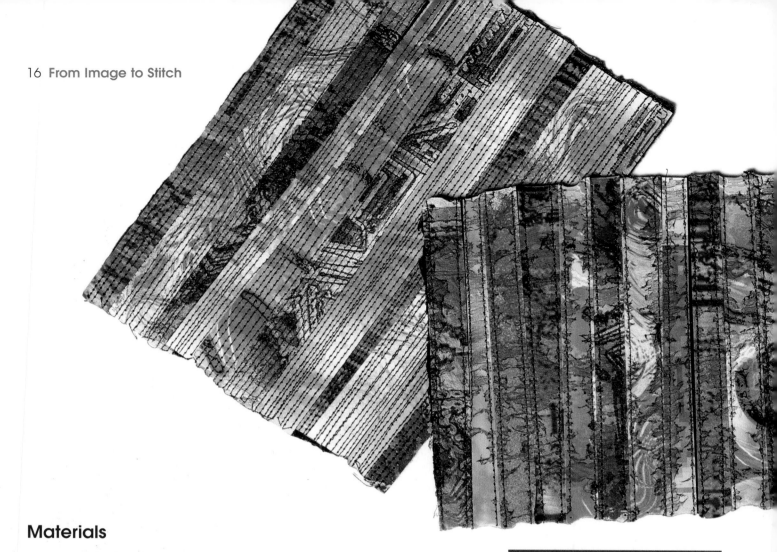

Materials

In this section we examine the use of printer paper, cartridge and Japanese papers, tissue and brown paper. They will happily go through the printer and provide a good surface for stitch. Much can be achieved with ordinary inkjet printer paper. Try using a coated 100g/m² paper, which is not too weighty and gives a good effect. Just print a design, choosing 'Best Quality' for the printer setting (see Appendix 2). Secure it to felt with 505 spray (temporary fabric adhesive) and then stitch straight lines over the top before cutting it into strips. A great addition to this process is to lay a chiffon scarf over the work before stitching and zap it afterwards with a heat tool.

Another ordinary paper is glossy photographic paper, which is very firm and makes great paper beads; vessels are another option. This paper is great for making up trial pieces to work through designs before constructing them as a textile. It can also be used to produce pieces of art in its own right, as shown opposite.

This will be fine for a quick result where the stitching is the main element but, if you want the printed image to have greater definition, there is an excellent product called InkAID that can be used with any paper or fabric to enhance the quality of the image. I prefer to use this product with paper but, if you don't wish to do so, you will achieve very acceptable images without it.

Previous page: This scroll was made by printing lettering on tissue paper and texturing it with zapped garden fleece. When bonded to craft Vilene, the tissue becomes stronger. A small image was applied to metal shim, using Rub-off Decals. Stitch was used to reinforce the paper and bring all the elements together.

Top: These two samples show how effective stitch can be when used to integrate printed images. The designs were printed on paper, mounted on heavy Vilene and stitched.

Above: Computer printouts are ideal for paper beads.

Below: These vessels were constructed from glossy photo paper. Some of the elements were stitched before folding and applying to the main body of the vessel. All pieces by Valerie Campbell-Harding.

InkAID

This amazing product allows you to print on anything that will go through your printer. It is designed to provide a surface similar to that used on expensive inkjet photographic paper and it gives a wonderful depth of colour to your images. It also means that you can print on fabric, lace, crumpled tissue paper and even metal, provided it is firmly stuck to a backing paper – more on that later.

Simply use a paintbrush to apply InkAID over the prepared paper and allow to dry for 24 hours. Dry as flat as possible by securing the coated paper to a piece of card and holding down the edges with bulldog clips.

It comes in different varieties:

- White Matte Precoat, which gives a flat, very white surface. It goes on clear but dries white.
- Clear Semi-Gloss Precoat, which allows you to coat the surface and preserve the colour or image underneath the Precoat. I find this very useful for printing on metal.
- Iridescent Precoats, which come in different finishes – gold, silvers, pearls – and can be pre-mixed with paints.
- Gloss Precoats, although I find the gloss too shiny for my purposes.

For paper, the best product is the White Matte Precoat, which works really well with paper and renders the piece lightfast too. You can see from the photographs opposite what a difference this product makes. I have used the Precoat for most of the pieces in this section but it is not essential and all the suggestions will work well without it.

Opposite: Comparison prints showing the difference that White Matte Precoat InkAID can make. These were both printed on watercolour paper but the one on the bottom was painted with InkAID and allowed to dry before printing.

Below: The InkAID product, which can make so much difference to inkjet prints.

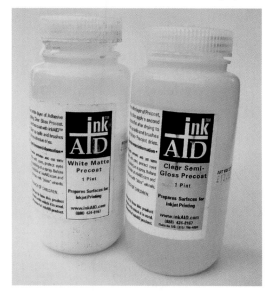

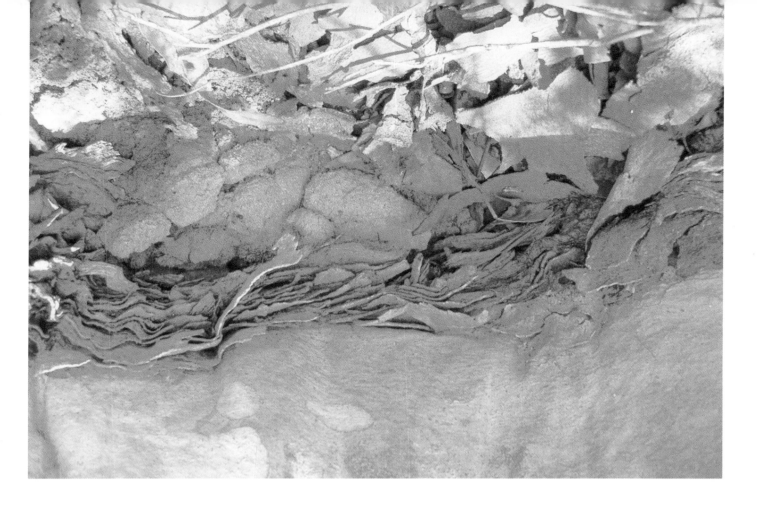

Cartridge paper

I like using sturdy art papers in my work; they are quick to print and give an immediate surface for stitching. It is also very easy to use them for combining mixed-media and paint effects with the printed surface. In the sample shown opposite, a digital photograph was distorted in a paint program. It was printed on cartridge paper coated in White Matte Precoat InkAID.

When printed, try the following:

1. Cut the paper into thick strips and place on dark felt.
2. Stitch into the paper strips from the back – the felt side. Consider the colour of the bobbin thread as this will show on the top. Automatic patterns (the ones built into the sewing machine) can be very effective. Even the utility patterns will create an interesting texture.
3. Weave the strips, or lay side by side on a suitable background.
4. Stitch the strips together by hand using a stab stitch, or with more machining. Create a focal point using metal shim, big beads or charms if the piece requires it.

Stitching the strips from the back pushes the felt up through the paper. Stitching on the paper side gives a flat effect that can be useful for some designs. It's amazing how much difference it makes. Try a sample, working both ways.

Extension techniques
- Gild the strips by brushing lightly with an almost-dry brush of metallic acrylic paint or use a metallic wax like Treasure Gold.
- Print the same design twice and weave together, leaving some of the strips unstitched.
- Edge some or all of the strips with dimensional paint to give interesting raised edges.

Black paper

One of the wonderful things about InkAID is the way that it allows you to print in colour on black paper. Something quite weighty is best, so use a reasonably heavy paper, equivalent to cartridge paper. You could print out the paper first – it will look odd on the black but you can just see the design lines. Then you can paint with White Matte Precoat InkAID, choosing which areas to leave black. Save the print layout in your paint program so that you can get the final print in exactly the same place. Print again when the InkAID is dry.

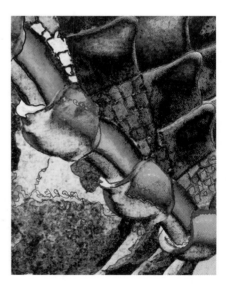

Above: This design, based on an image derived from Gaudí's architecture, was used for the pieces shown opposite.

Right: Try different weavings before stitching.

Below: The image was printed twice on cartridge paper. The papers were cut into strips and then stitched to dark felt. After they were woven together, more stitching was added.

Papers with mixed media

The weaving exercise will work with other papers, particularly the thicker handmade ones. It's interesting to combine inkjet-printed paper (don't forget to coat with InkAID first if it's an important piece) with other art media such as gesso or one of the many texture gels sold in art shops.

Here are some ideas:

- Use an inkpad and a rubber stamp with embossing powder to add raised metallic areas before weaving. This could be done on all the strips or just some of them.
- Draw along the edges of each strip with a dimensional paint like Tulip or Appliglue before weaving. Lay it on baking paper before running the applicator along the edge. Allow to dry before weaving.
- Instead of cutting and weaving the whole paper, cut slots through one area as shown in the design opposite. Print a second piece of paper and cut strips that relate to the slashed part of the image. Add some stitch and then sponge on some gesso to the strips to add texture. If the colour is wrong, paint the gesso with acrylics in a shade that matches your design. Dry and weave.
- Try the technique described above with a texture gel such as Liquitex Blended Fibres.

Above: A Gaudi-inspired design (shown on page 20) was printed on medium-weight black paper, coated in places with White Matte Precoat InkAID. Printing the design before coating with InkAID gave an idea of where the design elements should be placed on the page. This enabled judicious painting of the product to allow the black paper to show. It was stitched before the InkAID was applied.

Opposite: A digital photograph of a ruined chapel wall was used for this design, printed on heavy watercolour paper. Slits were cut in the paper and a further print was woven through one area. The print was then sponged with black gesso for added texture, and hand stitched. Eyelets were then added.

Japanese papers

Look out for other papers. Japanese papers – the very fine ones with holes – often work very well. I don't use InkAID on these as I find the coating destroys much of the fragile quality that I love. These papers are too fine to go through the printer on their own, so cut them to A4 size (30 × 21 cm, 11¾ × 8¼ inches) and use a glue stick around the edges (not all over) to apply them to normal printer paper – you can see how this works in the diagram. Make sure they are securely stuck all the way round the edge. It is possible to iron paper and fabric to freezer paper and put that through the printer but I find the glue-stick method better for paper.

When printed, you can carefully remove the Japanese paper from the backing paper. In fact, the effect when they are printed is very interesting as some of the print goes through the holes to the backing paper and this gives a sense of depth.

Here are some other ideas for this paper:

- Glue overlapping pieces of Japanese paper to a handmade paper and print on that. Make sure the pieces of paper are stuck down all round. Leave for a few hours and then lift some of the edges of the Japanese paper and gently apply a little metallic wax to the edges.
- Print and remove from the backing. Save the backing paper as it will have some printing on it. Tear the Japanese papers into strips and place on a background fabric – an embellished surface would be wonderful. Add further stitching.
- Try ink and bleach techniques, as the inkjet print will resist the bleach. Paint all over with black Quink ink and allow to dry. Dilute some household bleach and dab the inked papers with a sponge.

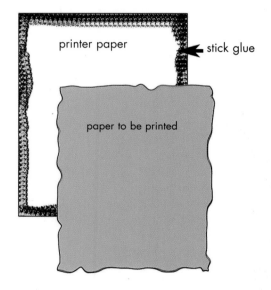

printer paper

stick glue

paper to be printed

Above: Fine paper can be applied to an ordinary printer paper by using a glue stick firmly around the edge of the printer paper. Place the fine paper on top and press down well. Allow the glue to dry.

Opposite: A fine Japanese paper was applied to printer paper, as shown in the diagram above. Part of the printing went through to the base paper and looked so good that it was decided to leave it in place. This piece could be enhanced by stitching.

Brown paper

Brown paper – the kind that you use for wrapping parcels – can be a great resource. Brown paper has a very special quality that comes into effect when it is crumpled. The thinner variety is best as the thicker type does not crumple well and it is this crumpling that makes the paper very like a fabric. It will become soft and pliable and lovely to stitch. When bonded to a backing, it is surprisingly hard wearing. Colour is affected by the paper colour, which gives a sepia-like quality to a print. Going for a black-and-white rather than a colour print will provide a sharper image.

I don't use InkAID on brown paper as I find that it masks its colour and texture.

Use a design that has lots of strong shapes – something geometric is ideal. Fine detail tends to get lost in the distressing process. Similarly, have lots of contrast with some blank areas so that the brown paper shows through. If you use a computer paint program, try using images from a copyright-free CD-ROM. You could build up borders and shapes to make an image like the one shown here.

Below: A design was taken from a Search Press CD-ROM on an Art Nouveau theme. This was manipulated in a paint program, using simple cut-and-paste commands.

Print on it in the same way that we used for the Japanese paper. Placing it on a sheet of ordinary printer paper (with glue stick around the edges) is a very good way to get it through the printer. When printed, leave it for an hour or so to set the ink and then crumple it up really well, being careful not to tear it. It should be very floppy and fabric-like at this stage.

Acrylic wax is a clear, water-based wax that can give a great finish to brown paper. Because it is water-based, it can cause the ink to run. Try ironing the print before crumpling, as this can sometimes set the inks and prevent them from running.

If you want to add interest before stitching,.try the following:

- Draw back into the image with metallic pens.
- Sponge with metallic paint.
- Lay a Distress Ink stamp-pad on the paper and press or drag it across the paper. These inks are not totally opaque and will allow the design to show through. They could be lightly sprinkled with embossing powder and heated to raise the surface.

Above left: The design was printed onto brown paper (using the carrier method described on page 24) and attached with Bondaweb to a firm Vilene base. The motif was outlined with free machining.

Above right: Some of these samples made for the book had black FuseFX ironed over the top.

Stitching the brown paper

The paper will need to be secured to a background and this is best done with Bondaweb (fusible webbing). Use a backing fabric, such as a strong cotton or felt, and iron Bondaweb onto it. Remove the paper and, while it is still warm, press the brown paper onto the webbing. Lay baking paper over the top and iron gently with a hot iron. Don't press or push the iron or you will iron out all the lovely crumples.

When this is done, you can stitch the brown paper by hand or machine. Here are some ideas:

- Iron onto acrylic felt and burn holes or shapes with a soldering iron. Or burn out strips with a soldering iron and mount them on a new backing.
- Use a large motif and cut, or burn, it out (so that there is a hole in the image). Place over a contrasting surface – perhaps a velvet. Free machine to secure the two materials. Highlight the shape by couching a machine-wrapped cord around the motif.
- Even if you have a printer that takes only relatively small sheets of paper, you can build up larger pieces by making brown paper-printed 'tiles' and stitching them to a background.

Below: Brown paper samples, all bonded to felt with painted Bondaweb ironed over the top.

Far left: The printed brown paper was bonded to felt, the underside of which had been foiled. It was then cut into segments, following the pattern, and wrapped pipe cleaners were couched along the edge of each segment. These were then curled up across the surface.

Middle and right: Further brown paper pieces, all with painted Bondaweb. Some are decorated by hand or machine.

Texturing with Bondaweb

Another good trick with the brown paper is to texture it by ironing onto painted Bondaweb (fusible webbing). Work like this:

1. Paint the adhesive side of Bondaweb with silk paint or Adirondack spray paint. If you wet it a little first by spraying or painting with water (don't get it too wet), the colour will be a faint wash, which is what we want.
2. When dry, iron it, painted side down, onto the crumpled brown paper. It's best to get it onto the backing fabric, as described opposite, before ironing the Bondaweb on top. Make sure that you lay baking paper between the iron and the painted Bondaweb. When adhered, remove the paper from the Bondaweb.
3. It's a fine line between applying too much heat and not enough, so experiment with your iron temperature and timing. It's probably best to err on the cooler side and finish off the heating with a heat tool.
4. The idea is to lay a wash of colour and texture over the brown paper. You may like this just as it is, but a little metallic wax, lightly applied, will pick up the texture. If you apply a sprinkling of embossing powder immediately after heating, it will stick to the warm webbing. Then use the minimum of heat with a heat tool.
5. Leave for 24 hours before stitching.

A similar product, like FuseFX or Mistyfuse, can be ironed onto the surface in the same way. If you use the black version of this, it will not need to be painted. Don't use the iron too hot or you will lose the crackled look.

Above: In the sample on the right, the brown paper has had fibres applied using an Embellisher machine (see page 37). The other samples show how an African-inspired design, by Ruth Issett, has undergone a colour change when printed on brown paper.

All of the stitching ideas discussed on the previous page will work with the Bondaweb-textured paper. Bear in mind that you are adding colour with the Bondaweb, so it can be interesting to use this over a monoprinted (black ink only) image.

Above: Printed brown paper with holes torn into it was bonded to dark felt. Scraps of walnut-dyed lace and lines of satin stitch were then added. Valerie Campbell-Harding.

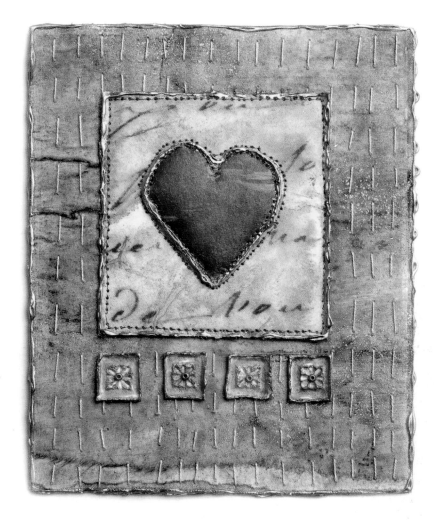

Tissue paper

Tissue paper is a wonderful material for image transfer. Although it is very fragile, it can be applied to a backing fabric with Bondaweb fusible webbing, which gives it considerable strength, although it does mean it isn't fully washable. Using InkAID makes the image sharper and brighter. However, this may not be desirable if you are after a pale, distressed image, so judge each print individually according to the result that best suits the work. It's great for getting effects with lettering.

The nature of the paper – the way it can be crumpled and distressed – makes it a wonderful material for portraying old parchment, faded frescos or icons. Treated in another way, it can achieve the look of leather. As a paper, it can be stamped, inked, bleached, sprayed and gilded – before or after printing. The reverse of the print can be sprayed with gold paint to give a subtle shimmer to the image. What a treasure! Consider which images to print to make the most of this versatile material. Even if you are not into computer design, you could use a word processor with a suitable font and place some letters for a manuscript piece. Find icons on the Internet (check copyright), and photograph frescos or old walls with your digital camera. Then just print it out as described overleaf.

Printing on tissue paper

Print your image using the glue-stick and printer-paper method (see page 24). Peel or tear it away from the backing paper, crumple it very gently and transfer it like this:

1. Cut a piece of craft Vilene or white felt to the size required; slightly under A4 (30 × 21cm, 11¾ × 8¼ inches) is a good size to start with.
2. Cut a piece of Bondaweb slightly smaller than the Vilene.
3. Iron the Bondaweb onto the Vilene and pull away the paper backing.
4. While the surface is still warm and slightly tacky, press the tissue-paper print onto it, creasing a little as you go.
5. Finally, place baking paper over the surface and iron it once more with a hot iron.

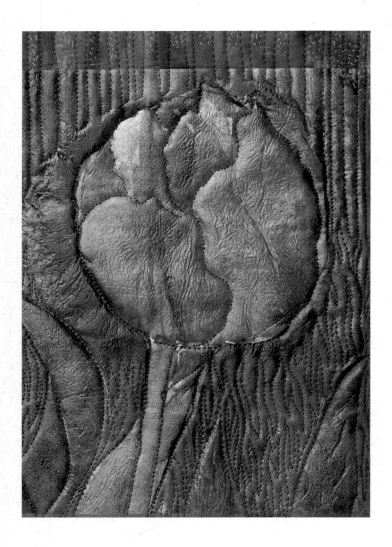

Opposite: *Tulip: Through a Glass Darkly*
39 x 63 cm (15 x 25 inches)
The background for his lovely quilt was hand-dyed cotton. The central area was made from a print on InkAID-treated Tissutex. This was bonded to the background and machine quilted with hand-stitched embellishment.
Marie Roper.

Left: In the detail, you can see the texture of the tissue paper.

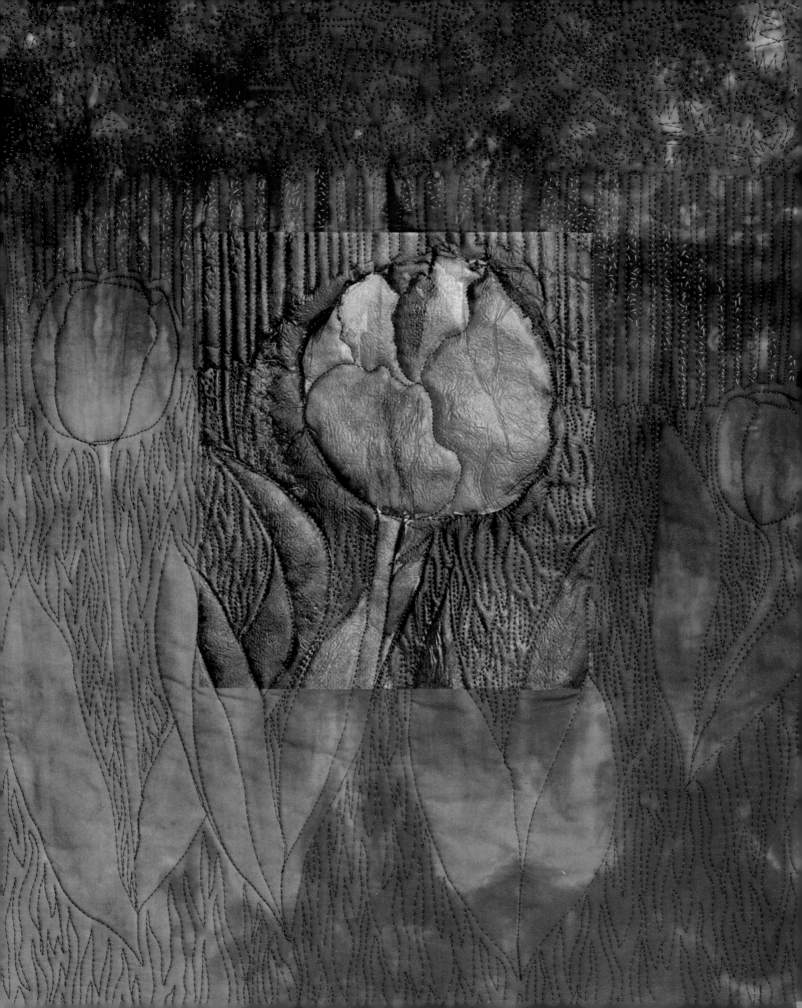

Special effects

The basic image can be enhanced using some additional materials:

- Iron painted Bondaweb over the image, as before.
- Spray the back of the tissue paper with metallic spray paint. Allow to dry before crumpling and bonding to a background.
- Print on the image using dark puff paint and a stamp. Use a heat tool to raise the surface. Try a little metallic wax or a dry brush of gold paint to highlight the texture of the puff paint.
- Use Paper Perfect in a toning colour in certain areas of the image, especially if you are after a distressed manuscript effect. Gesso can have a similar effect when a fresco-like surface is required.
- Spray with black webbing spray – great for an ageing effect. Or use a Moon Shadow Mist spray, squirting gently so that drips form.
- Dab on some Quink ink in places and discharge with a little dilute bleach (see page 24).

Below: Crumpled tissue paper was applied to felt and stamped with charcoal puff paint. This was gilded by lightly rubbing with a Markal (Shiva) Oilbar. Thick embossing powder was melted in a ladle (use a heat tool underneath the ladle) or Melting Pot and dripped onto the surface.

Using a word processor with tissue paper

It is quite possible to use a very basic word processor for
printing text on tissue paper. Some of these ideas work well:

- The Symbol font could be used (select a large font size)
  to add motifs as well as text.
- The tissue could be painted first, using watercolours or
  walnut inks. Allow to dry before pasting the edges onto a
  carrier sheet. Then print as before.
- Unpainted tissue could be printed with a word processor,
  torn into strips and bonded to a background. It could
  then have coloured Tissutex (abaca tissue) bonded over
  the top of it.

Above: Text can be used to good effect.
Here, a 'do-list' was printed on tissue paper
using a word-processing program.
Bondaweb (fusible webbing) was ironed
onto felt and torn pieces of the print placed
on top. Baking paper was placed over it
and the torn pieces were applied. Then,
dyed abaca tissue was ironed over the top.
The pieces were hand stitched ready to
become backgrounds. The piece on the
right was stamped before stitching and a
little gold foil was added.

Adding texture and stitch to tissue prints

Even more texture can be added by stitching or embellishing into tissue.

- Paint a piece of agricultural fleece or nappy (diaper) liner. Use walnut ink for a manuscript look or dilute silk paint for colour. When dry, stitch it on top of the image using straight lines of stitch. Add some Markal (Shiva) oilbar and zap with a heat tool. An alternative is to machine automatic patterns over it.
- Make a chiffon sandwich and stitch over the image. Make sure that you use the fine scarf chiffon. Here's how:
  1. Iron Bondaweb onto a piece of chiffon. Use baking paper and don't have the iron too hot.
  2. Iron Transfoil lightly over the Bondaweb and then place the second piece of chiffon on top. Cover with baking parchment and iron.
  3. Place strips of this sandwich over the background and work a pattern or free machine over it before zapping with a heat tool.

Below left: Detail of the scroll shown in full below right and also featured on page 14. You can see in the detail how the agricultural fleece, which was bonded over the tissue print, adds texture and a semblance of age.

Below right: The scroll shown in full.

Using an Embellisher machine

The printed tissue could be used on an Embellisher (needle felting) machine but printed tissue or Tissutex is difficult to embellish as there are no fibres to be pulled through the fabric. The secret is to work on commercial felt as a backing, lay on the tissue and then place a chiffon scarf on top. Embellish this sandwich and the chiffon will go through the paper, fixing it firmly. If the chiffon is too heavy, use a heat tool to zap some of it away. I like to add fibres to the tissue so that the pattern peeps out in places. You can see the effect in the vessel shown here.

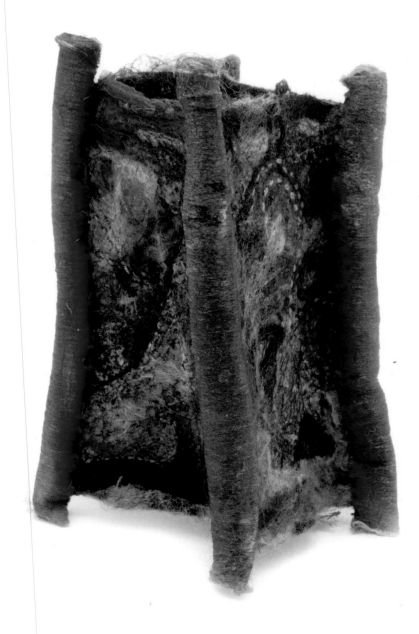

Above and left: Printed abaca tissue, which is slightly stronger than ordinary tissue, was applied to a surface using an Embellisher machine. The surface was prepared by laying down silk fibres on felt and running the machine over it. Then the tissue was applied in the same way and, finally, very sheer chiffon was Embellished over the top to anchor it all down. The detail shows the effect of the printed tissue with hand stitching. The material was then made into a vessel with silk carrier rods forming the sides.

They will not learn.
They will perish

Forests in Canada
destroyed

Global warming
Stop de-forestation

They will not learn
They will perish

Polar icecaps melting
Flood Flood Flood

Global warming
Stop de-forestation

Polar icecaps melting
Flood Flood Flood

Global warming
Stop de-forestation

Forests in Canada
destroyed

Tissue paper on metal

A really exciting effect that only tissue paper can give is created by fixing the tissue print onto metal. This could embrace the idea of recycling by using the insides of tomato purée tubes or aluminium cans. Best of all is very thin copper shim (0.05 mm) which can be heated in a flame until it changes colour. If you use a fine tissue paper, this coloration will show through. This technique is especially effective if the tissue is torn and some of the metal is allowed to show. This can be embossed from the back with a pen or embossing tool to form areas of pattern. It makes great greetings cards.

1. Print out as described previously and remove the tissue from the backing paper.
2. Prepare the metal; the piece shown here has been heated in a gas flame first.
3. The tissue is laid, face down, on baking paper and Bondaweb is ironed onto the back. The paper is removed and then the tissue and Bondaweb are ironed onto the metal. Don't forget to use baking paper between the iron and the tissue.
4. Leave it for a day or two until it ceases to be sticky. Draw a line with an embossing tool or pen at the point where the print ends. Don't press too hard.
5. Now place it face down over a magazine or mouse mat and draw into the metal – you will see where to start by the embossed line. You could use a planned pattern or just mark-making lines, dots and dashes.
6. If you wish to add stitch, always place the metal on heavy interfacing or felt and make sure that you are working on fine metal, not too thick. This should prevent thread breakage. Work patterns or free running stitches.
7. Finally, paint a thin coat of matt acrylic varnish over the surface of the paper. This will make it very hard-wearing.

This is a super technique, one I use a lot, and you will soon see plenty of possibilities. Large textiles can be built up by pasting lots of tissue prints to a bigger piece of metal. Alternatively, many small tissued metal pieces could be applied to a background fabric and joined by free-machine stitching.

Opposite: *Power Hungry World*. Printed tissue was applied to thin metal shim, working from research notes and photographs of the effects of global warming, particularly in Canada. The three pieces were stitched to a base of black felt and machine embroidery was used to highlight some areas. Some of the tissue was scraped back to show the metal. Finally, little notes were printed on hand-made paper and glued to the base.

Texture

Textured surfaces can be built up using paper and stitch. Khadi paper (or any of the Indian papers that have the look of handmade paper) will work well but you may need to use a firm cotton backing as a stabilizer when stitching heavily on the paper. Consider applying fabrics that have been textured using an Embellisher machine. They could be free machined to a paper base for a heavily textured look, or maybe use soft leather or zapped felt for a really heavy texture.

InkAID collages

InkAID is good for adding texture, too. Collage effects can be made and printed after coating.

The image on page 42 came from a digital photograph of colourful pots in a shady garden. It was distorted using an effect from an image-preparation program. A piece of printer paper with bands of lace and torn pieces of kitchen paper firmly stuck to it was painted with InkAID – you can see what great texture was obtained when this was printed.

Some printers will leave marks on the print when you use InkAID on a textured surface. This is what's known as the 'pizza wheel effect', caused by the mechanism that pushes the paper through. There is a lot on the website – see details in the 'Useful Stuff' section – about how to avoid these but I have never found it a particular problem as, with the sort of textiles we use, anything like that tends to be stitched into the surface. Wonderful surfaces can be built up, perhaps with stitching, and then printed.

Making a collaged surface for InkAID

This is quite a bumpy surface and you may want to use an old printer. I haven't had any problems but can't guarantee that they won't occur. Work like this:

1. Take an ordinary piece of printer paper – this will be your base – and stick little pieces of lace, kitchen roll maybe and even the odd bit of chiffon to that. Use a glue stick or any sort of glue that will hold it down firmly but make sure it is dry before printing.
2. Coat it with the White Matte Precoat and leave it to dry for 24 hours. It may need two coats but I have found that to be unusual.
3. When it is quite dry, put it through the printer with your printer set to the High Resolution setting. When it is complete, you will have your image on a wonderfully textured surface.

You may find that this is too stiff to hand stitch but it should be fine on the machine and could be wonderful used with the weaving techniques we looked at earlier. Sometimes these pieces can stand alone as artworks.

Above and opposite: This computer design was built up from drawn studies of a fence. The drawing was scanned into the computer and special effects were used to raise some areas of the design. The result, shown opposite, was printed on watercolour paper with soft, padded leathers worked over the top. Jane Lemon.

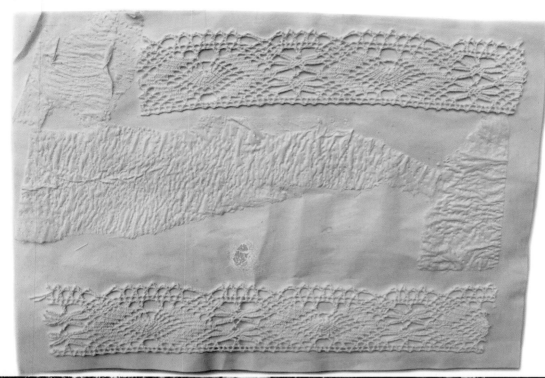

Left: The base for the Majorelle piece. Lace and kitchen paper were glued to printer paper and coated with InkAID. They were then printed using an inkjet printer.

Below: An InkAID collage, this textile started life as a digital photograph of the Majorelle gardens in Marrakech, Morocco. It was printed on ordinary printer paper onto which had been glued lace and torn kitchen paper. This was then painted with White Matte Precoat InkAID before printing. It gives a great texture but care had to be taken when putting it through the printer.

Using InkAID with metal

The Semi-gloss InkAID is wonderful when used with metal, but you may wonder how on earth you are going to get your metal through the printer. I use fine metal shim (0.05 mm). Try the following to get a really good print onto your metal:

1. Coat the shim with the Semi-gloss InkAID. Allow to dry. Make sure that the metal is really clean. I usually wipe it over with nail polish remover to remove any grease. Allow to dry before you coat it with the product.
2. Let the InkAID dry well and apply a second coat.
3. Take a piece of ordinary printer paper and tape the piece of shim onto it using heavy tape so that it sticks well all round.
4. Put it through the printer. I have not had any problems putting this through an ordinary printer but can't be responsible for any problems you may have. If you are at all unsure then use the decals (see page 46) or the tissue method (page 32).

Printers are so cheap nowadays that you may consider buying a simple, basic printer to use for experimenting, if you get really hooked. In the meantime, as long as you don't put anything in that is too chunky, you will find most things go through well. After all, your printer takes quite thick card and there is no reason why it shouldn't take this. The InkAID products won't flake or damage your printer when used in this way.

Right: InkAID can be used on fine metal shim if it is firmly taped to paper. It gives a good finish. The sample shown here was a drawing of a grave painting, scanned into a paint program. Angel details for another project were added so that none of the shim was wasted.

You will be able to stitch into the metal when the ink is really, really dry. Be sure to place the shim over thick Vilene before stitching or the thread will break. Stitch to add highlights or, perhaps, use pattern over some areas only. Use it as a focal point over printed tissue on Vilene.

Left: The printed metal shim shown on the previous page was placed on heavy Vilene interfacing and stitched. The resulting embroidery was used as a centrepiece in this textile. The backing was a tissue-paper print, bonded to Vilene and stitched with padded kid leather and couched metallic thread.

Opposite: The design used for these two textiles was based on drawings of angels in the Watts Chapel, near Guildford, Surrey. Designed by Mary Seton Watts, the wonderful decoration combines an Art Nouveau theme with Celtic designs and interlacings. The design on the left was stitched on Fuzzy Paper, using free running stitch. It was then repeated for the piece on the right, on a surface of eggshells glued to Vilene, using Dry Rub-off Decals (see page 46).

Speciality papers

It is possible to buy inkjet versions of many art papers in a huge variety of weights, but this book focuses on easy-to-find paper that can be used for stitch. However, I can't leave this section without mentioning three products that I find exciting. They are all sold by Crafty Computer Paper – see 'Useful Stuff'.

Fuzzy Paper

This produces a wonderful velvet-like print that is great for stitched surfaces. At first sight it doesn't look too promising as it has a paper backing but, in practice, this seems to make no difference. Just print in the usual way, lay on a firm surface – felt works best for me – and machine stitch to enhance the design. Note that the thickness of the felt will cause it to quilt a little.

The piece shown right was taken from a photograph of the Watts Chapel, Guildford, Surrey. This chapel has wonderful painted angels, which I photographed and then drew and painted. They came out really well on the Fuzzy Paper.

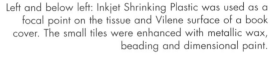

Left and below left: Inkjet Shrinking Plastic was used as a focal point on the tissue and Vilene surface of a book cover. The small tiles were enhanced with metallic wax, beading and dimensional paint.

Below: Tassel. Dry Rub-Off Decals were used to colour the metal shim, which was then beaded and stitched. Hazel Credland and Lynn Horniblow (detail on page 127).

Shrinking Plastic

This is an inkjet version of the usual Shrinky Plastic. You print on it, cut out the motifs and use a heat tool to make them shrink, thicken and intensify in colour.

Be aware that the colours darken significantly, so use light colours in your designs. I do find these motifs useful for accents, especially work based on illuminated manuscripts, where they make wonderful initial letters. Remember to make holes (with a hole punch) before shrinking them. I like to make tiles with holes in each corner. These can be disguised by a bead.

Dry Rub-Off Decals

I am totally hooked on this decal paper. Although it doesn't sound very inspiring it can be used on anything and is wonderful on metal, wood or leather. It goes easily through any printer, too. It is a sticky business and a little time-consuming. Full instructions are given with the product and it does involve a lot of sticking and peeling. My best advice, when you get to the final sticky stage, is to peel the top of the print away from its final backing, place this on the surface and then gradually peel the rest away. Otherwise try tweezers to place the sticky decal on the metal.

Above: More of the decals, showing the wide range of surfaces that they can enhance. Here, they are shown on metal shim, silver kid and brown paper. Also shown is a tissued sample with cast paper raising the surface. The decal covers this raised surface, giving an interesting effect.

Rub-away techniques

Here we look at products that involve coating the printed image to form a seal, after which the backing paper is washed away. In this way, the image is revealed through the coated surface. The advantage is that, in general, the products are good value for money. Although they may not be suitable for making garments (the surface can be quite stiff), they can provide very sharp details, which are great for use in books, bags, vessels or wall-hangings. I find that using them on surfaces such as craft Vilene or felt gives a less shiny finish. Photocopies make for clear images as inkjet prints tend to run a little. However, this effect can provide an intriguing distressed surface.

Several methods are suggested here, some using commercial products and others making use of less conventional media for some special effects.

Opposite: Detail of Sandra Meech quilt shown in full on page 51.

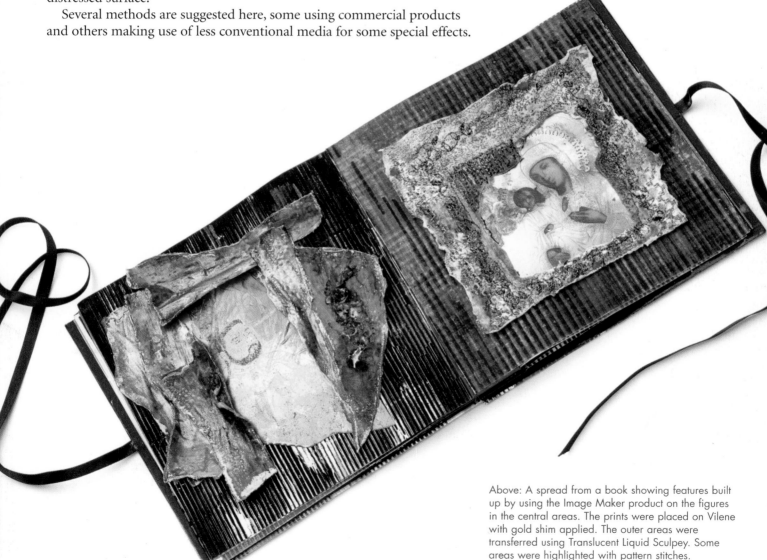

Above: A spread from a book showing features built up by using the Image Maker product on the figures in the central areas. The prints were placed on Vilene with gold shim applied. The outer areas were transferred using Translucent Liquid Sculpey. Some areas were highlighted with pattern stitches.

Materials

You will, I'm sure, recognize many of the brands that are sold for this purpose: Image Maker, Picture This, Translucent Liquid Sculpey and so on. All of these products involve coating the image to seal it and then removing the backing paper by wetting it and rubbing it away. Other ideas that will be considered give more distressed, less perfect results. These involve the use of Bondaweb.

If you are using photocopies, bear the following points in mind:

- Make sure that your original images are as good as possible, and use high-quality paper and the highest printer setting, such as 'Best Photo'.
- Remember that the design will be reversed, so always reverse it either on the photocopier or before you print it out.
- Using a photocopier is a good way of increasing the size of the work so that you are not always confined to standard-sized, small images – you could have your image enlarged as it is photocopied or you could make a collage of images on a larger sheet of paper before using the photocopier.

Picture This

This is one of the best of the rub-away mediums. Work with a photocopy because photocopy paper is more waterproof. Take your inkjet image down to the photocopy shop and have a copy made. It goes very well onto a heavy Vilene; I use the craft weight. On this material, it does not seem to be so 'plasticky' and can easily be hand stitched as desired.

The usual rule when painting the product onto your image is that the larger the image you are transferring, the thicker the layer. The instructions say that the image should be a small one but I have worked with bigger sizes with no problems. With large images you have to work faster as the product may dry out. Heat may also affect the drying rate.

Below: Some of the materials that can be used for rub-away techniques.

Method

1. Wash and dry your fabric to remove any finish that it may hold and then put a protective backing underneath. Cut to the size required and then paint the paste onto the picture and spread it evenly over the surface with a clean brush. It should be thick enough so that it obscures the picture underneath.

2. Lift up your picture and place it face-side down on your piece of fabric on a hard surface protected with baking paper. Press down very evenly to make sure there aren't any wrinkles and then place a paper towel or kitchen paper over the transfer and roll it with a brayer or rolling pin in opposite directions for at least a minute. This will ensure that all the surface has adhered. Then remove the towel and take away any excess product from around the edges.

3. Let it dry thoroughly for 48 hours, if possible. When it is dry, place a water-soaked sponge onto the transfer and soak the paper so that it is really soft. Remove the sponge and leave it for a little while so that the softening-up process continues. Then, using your finger or an eraser, rub away the paper. Keep rubbing until you can see your print underneath. You will probably need to dampen the paper layers underneath again, so you can use the water-soaked sponge or the water spray as before.

4. When it is dry, rub off any paper that may be left, using the sponge, if necessary. Make sure that all the paper is removed. Don't wash it for 72 hours; after that it is safe to wash at 30°C.

Right: A quilt on a theme of Man's destruction of the Canadian forests. Each of the squares shows design work that has been photocopied and transferred to fabric using the Picture This medium.
Sandra Meech.

Above: The Image Maker product was used to transfer the maps and photos for the cover of this book, which contains details of the author's grandfather and the diary he kept during World War 1.

You may find that this gives you a slightly plasticized coating that is difficult to stitch other than by machine. It will be fine as a background for appliqué. Try applying such things as water-soluble stitching, embellished surfaces or areas of machine embroidery.

Image Maker
This is much cheaper than Picture This and is usually easy to find in haberdashery stores or hobby shops. It has a tendency to rub off when you rub away the paper and the detail is not so crisp. Work in exactly the same way as before.

Suggestions for stitch

With all of these products there are various ways of extending the technique. Adding or adapting fabrics and trying different stitch methods can add a new dimension.

Here are a few suggestions:
- Stitch the fabric first and then use that for the base.
- Tear the photocopy into strips before transferring and place it onto a pale-coloured fabric.
- Do not paint the medium over the entire image – leave gaps for effect.
- Scratch away some of the print for a distressed effect.

Translucent Liquid Sculpey (TLS)

This is a relative of polymer clay and it does, in fact, seal a very thin layer of clay over the image, which is then baked in an oven, ironed or heat treated with a heat tool to set the clay. It is a very versatile medium that allows for some interesting diversions. Here's the basic method.

1. Take your photocopy and paint the surface with a thin layer of TLS.
2. Bake in an oven at the suggested temperature or allow to dry and then iron, with baking paper between the TLS and the iron. Alternatively, play a heat tool over the surface, not allowing the heat to linger in any one spot. Do not overheat this medium – read the label.
3. When cooked, wet and rub as before.

Here are some extensions for this technique:

- Use an inkjet image that will smudge slightly.
- At the rub-off stage leave some paper on the back; this will give a matt image that will be slightly uneven.
- Set some silk fibres or fine chiffon on top of the TLS at the runny stage.
- Mix Paper Perfect with the TLS when painting it onto the image.
- Colour with alcohol inks.

Above: *The Presence of Angels*.
This little piece was made using a stamp and embossing powder. Layers of inkjet-printed paper were sponged with metallic paint and coated with Translucent Liquid Sculpey. They were then hand stitched together. The snippets of text refer to angels and were made using the Translucent Liquid Sculpey transfer method. The central angel figure was made from an angel stamp and embossing powder.

Using Bondaweb for transfers

Bondaweb (fusible webbing), which is normally used to fuse fabrics together, can also be used to transfer photocopied or printed images. Inkjet prints may smudge – which is sometimes just the effect that is required. Otherwise, just take your inkjet image to the copy shop and have a colour print made.

This method of transferring designs is not suitable for anything that will need to be washed. However, it is wonderful for a pale, distressed look as a certain amount of paper usually remains, coating the top of the Bondaweb. The fractured quality of the images makes them very suitable for portraying faded frescos, icons or ancient books – anywhere that you need a pale, faded image. You could even try painting the Bondaweb very, very lightly with a dilute solution of walnut ink before you do the transfer. Look at the back of the fabric opposite – you'll find a lovely Impressionist-like painting.

Choose a clear, sharp image and, if working with an inkjet printer, use a good paper but not one that is too thick. The basic idea is to iron Bondaweb onto a prepared fabric and then iron on a colour print or photocopy, face down. The paper is then dampened and peeled away, leaving the image on top of the webbing.

Work like this:

1. Place your fabric on an ironing board and iron the Bondaweb onto it, using a hot iron. Peel the backing paper off. Now cut away any spare paper from your image and iron it, face down, onto the Bondaweb. Iron really well, and then spray water over it. If you plunge the whole thing into water it's likely to streak, and I find much the best way is to trim away as much paper as possible and then spray it with a water sprayer.
2. When the top surface of the paper is damp, leave it for a short while until the water has just soaked in, then rub away with your fingers or an eraser until you have removed a layer of paper. Dampen again if necessary and rub down to your image, most of which will have adhered to the Bondaweb.
3. To extend the technique you could try leaving a little of the paper on the top and drawing with Graphitint pencils while it is still a little damp.

Right: The small colourful areas in this bangle were made from Bondaweb transfers on craft Vilene. These were stitched by outlining the design with free-machine stitches and then mounting them on a strip of black felt. Water-soluble fabric, stitched with metallic thread, forms an eye-catching edging.

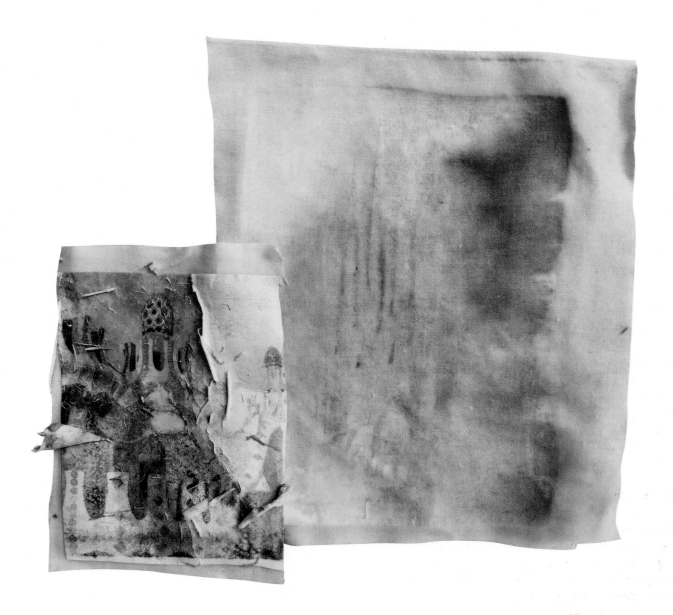

Above: Bondaweb was used to transfer a digital photo to fabric. Extra water was added, which had the effect of washing the print through to the back of the fabric to give the appearance of an Impressionist painting.

Left: Drawing into the Bondaweb (fusible webbing) transfer with Graphitint pencils gives an interesting effect.

This works particularly well with sketchbook images, especially when you are looking at architecture. Try using it with your holiday photographs, where a digital image printed onto Bondaweb can be wonderful, especially when made into a book.

In this section we've explored lots of ways to use printed paper – from tissue to Picture This. Paper is an easy, natural material to put through your printer. These ideas are very much a starting point – experiment and have fun.

Below: A concertina book was filled with images of Barcelona, transferred to fabric using the Bondaweb method. The images were then enhanced with Graphitint pencils before being stitched by hand and machine.

Summary of techniques

Product	For	Against	Best For
InkAID	Greatly improves image quality. Possible to print on a huge variety of surfaces.	Thickens paper. Can be difficult to get through printer. Mail order.	Textured surfaces, collage work. Printing on metal.
Brown paper	Cheap. Good texture.	Needs support through printer.	Bonding to paper. Adding texture with Bondaweb.
Tissue paper Tissutex	Readily available. Cheap.	Needs support. Fragile until bonded.	Great for manuscripts. Good on Embellisher machine. Strong when bonded. Good texture when crumpled.
Speciality papers (Crafty Computer Papers)	Easy to print. Can be fiddly to use (Decals). Variety of effects obtainable.	Can be expensive. Some have long drying times.	Rub-off Decals are fantastic on metal. Shrinking Plastic is fun to use. Fuzzy Paper has great texture.
Image Maker	Cheap. Widely available.	Needs photocopier. Can be rubbed off. Not easy to hand stitch. Long preparation time.	Best on craft Vilene.
Picture This	Sharp image. Hard-wearing.	Expensive. Needs photocopier. Slightly plastic effect. Mail order only. Long preparation time.	Good for bags, vessels and machine stitch. Effective with lettering.
Liquid Translucent Sculpey	Good for special effects. Not too shiny.	Stiff — hard to hand stitch.	Exciting effects with trappings. Transluscent effect – good for layering or placing on metal.
Bondaweb (fusible webbing)	In the cupboard; not expensive.	Can cause paint to run.	Wonderful distressed effect; good with added media.

Section 2
Print on Fabrics

A wide variety of ready-to-print fabrics can be purchased, all treated to make them colourfast and lightfast. It is also possible to buy a solution in which to soak your own fabrics to provide these qualities, or to paint on a special finish before printing. The ready-to-print fabrics available range from sheer fabrics to cottons and they are simplicity itself to use. They are often mounted on paper, which is simply fed through the printer. They are washable, with care, and have excellent lightfast qualities. Although expensive, they are well worth the investment when you consider the time and effort put into a textile artwork. The fabrics can also be purchased by the metre for larger pieces; this possibility is examined later in the book.

This section looks at ways of using these fabrics as well as at using photographs and getting designs into the computer. Many design methods, such as clingfilm prints and sgraffito techniques, work well on paper but not at all on fabric. Such techniques are ideal subjects for the print and stitch methods described here.

Fabric choice

The choice of available fabrics is getting wider all the time and the finish is generally excellent. What to choose? Cotton is a popular choice – a good smooth fabric that produces a crisp print, just asking for further enhancement in the way of stitching. Silk, with its lustrous sheen, is an exciting fabric, and the sheer fabric offers opportunity for layering. Organza or voile bring their own translucent qualities.

Transferring designs onto these print-ready fabrics gives excellent results as the fabric handle is not affected and the prints can easily be stitched by hand or machine.

Materials

Print-ready fabrics are available from many suppliers – you will find them listed under 'Useful Stuff'. They all differ slightly and you will find your favourite by trial and error. Some give a very true reproduction, some seem over-bright, others a little dull. All those listed under 'Useful Stuff' work well. In every case, your printer setting will have a bearing on the end result, so check the instructions that come with the fabrics. Do remember this check, as some of the fabrics require ironing after printing to set the ink.

You can make your own print-ready sheets by using Bubble Jet Set 2000. With this product, the fabric is soaked and dried before printing. It is not as good as the best of the commercial ones but is quite satisfactory for textiles that will have a lot of stitching. Some fabrics react better than others, so do some trials before launching into a large piece of work. There is more on this product later in this section.

Using the fabrics

Set the printer to high resolution or 'Best Quality'. Some fabrics may be slightly wider than the standard A4 size (30 × 21 cm, 11¾ × 8¼ in), so ensure that the paper guides are set for this – otherwise the fabric print may be crooked. These fabrics are suitable for use with any design source – photos from digital cameras, sketchbook designs, computer-generated images or scanned artwork. This section looks at ideas for stitching with these images and also includes some ways of producing the images themselves.

Previous page: *Little Italy* (detail) Print-ready cotton was used to transfer this sketchbook image from an Italian holiday. This was then placed on felt and machine stitched. Paper impressions of carnival masks were applied.

Opposite: *Maternity*. This work was produced to welcome a new addition to the family. The pre-birth ultrasound recording was scanned into the computer and printed on cotton fabric. The use of painted eggshells was an appropriate background. Siân Martin.

Below: Ready-to-print fabrics save a lot of time and come in a good range of materials.

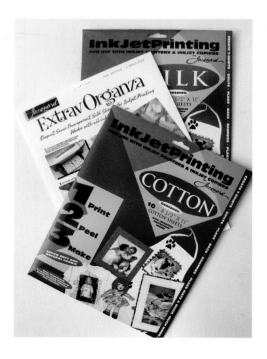

Image capture

Use a digital camera, sketchbook or other sources to obtain images to form the basis of exciting designs.

Digital photographs

The immediacy of a digital camera can be a wonderful asset and often a suitable subject can be found in your own garden. The photograph can be printed out straight from the camera and enhanced with machine embroidery or quilting but, with just a little extra effort, it can be 'tweaked' in a design program. The photographs below show how a simple flower study can be turned into something much more special with just one special effect.

Holiday photographs can be an excellent reminder of a wonderful trip. Consider making a hanging that combines several aspects of the holiday destination or different places visited during a touring holiday. Perhaps something practical could be constructed – maybe a covered box file containing holiday souvenirs, a book cover or photo album.

Below and opposite: *Blue Flower*
A closely cropped digital photograph of a white *magnolia stellata* flower was edited in Virtual Painter and printed onto inkjet cotton fabric. Using reverse appliqué, several layers of organza were free-machined to outline the petals of the flower and cut back to reveal the delicate colours. The embroidery was then mounted onto a textured velvet background.
Hazel Credland.

Distorting a photograph

Val Campbell-Harding showed me a wonderful technique for making background fabrics using a digital camera. She called them 'swoopy backgrounds' and they are quite easy once you have mastered the trick.

Here's what you do:

1. Find out from the camera's manual how to adjust the EV (Exposure Value) setting. Try going up a couple of settings to let in more light. Alternatively, find the menu – or mode – that offers such settings as landscape, movement etc. and choose the one for night photographs.
2. Select a colourful subject, perhaps a bright herbaceous border or a wall with lots of posters.
3. Start to move the camera in a steady swoop, pressing the shutter button at the same time. You may have to try this several times but, at least with digital cameras, the picture can be deleted. You should achieve an interesting flowing image with gently blurred colours – similar to the one shown centre right.

Consider using a paint or imaging program to add further enhancements to the resulting photograph. The subject of the distorted photograph shown here was some colourful peonies (top right). The resulting swoop was given definition by using an 'Inked Edges' filter and then distorted with a special effect called 'Polar Co-ordinates' (bottom right). You may not have the same effects but it is worth experimenting with your software.

The subject of the images on these two pages were some garden peonies (top). A 'swoopy' photograph (middle) was taken with the menu set for night-time photography. The camera is moved in a smooth swoop as the shutter is depressed. The design produced was used as a background for text before a paint program special effect (Polar Co-ordinates) was used to give this exciting design (bottom).

The design was printed on both cotton and ExtravOrganza as a base for hand and machine stitching.

Sketchbook designs

A sketchbook is a powerful image maker. Even rough sketches can be built up using a paint or image-manipulation program.

A series of rough sketches formed the basis of the 'Little Italy' panel, shown opposite. Hastily scribbled in a small sketchbook during an Italian holiday, they were scanned into the computer and joined together to form a long thin shape that could be printed on two pieces of A4 (30 × 21 cm, 11¾ × 8¼ inches) paper. The outline design was filled in using a paint program. The paintbrush opacity was reduced to produce a soft pastel effect. It could just as easily have been coloured by hand and scanned in.

Print-ready cotton was then used for the print. This was placed on felt and machine stitched. Paper impressions of carnival masks, made using a rubber stamp, were then applied.

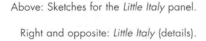

Above: Sketches for the *Little Italy* panel.

Right and opposite: *Little Italy* (details).

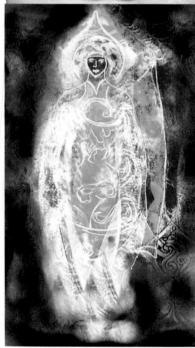

Top: This design started out as a drawing of angels in the Watts Chapel, Guildford, Surrey. The colours were reversed using the 'Negative' command, giving this ethereal image, bottom.

Computer-generated images

We have looked briefly at some ways of enhancing or distorting images. Paint programs are not expensive and some of the better ones are listed in the 'Useful Stuff' section. Some can even be downloaded free of charge. Image-manipulation programs can produce good results but over-use of the special effects can produce some rather predictable ones.

Here are a few ideas for producing something a little different:

- Use two or three effects, one on top of the other. This gives a more complex image than one easily recognized effect used alone.
- Try some of the colour commands. Most of us work within our colour comfort range; changing to Negative in the colour menu is good for us!
- If you only use one effect, look for something called Displacement Map in the Distort menu of your software and try to master it. The logic behind it allows an abstract image, perhaps one with just colours, to take on the shape of another image – the one used as a map. In doing so, fabulous textures are created. The map image can be another of your own images or one built into the program. You need an image with high contrasts to be the map. Look at diagrams overleaf to see what I mean.

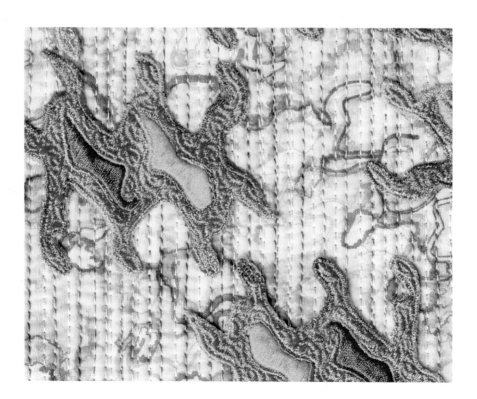

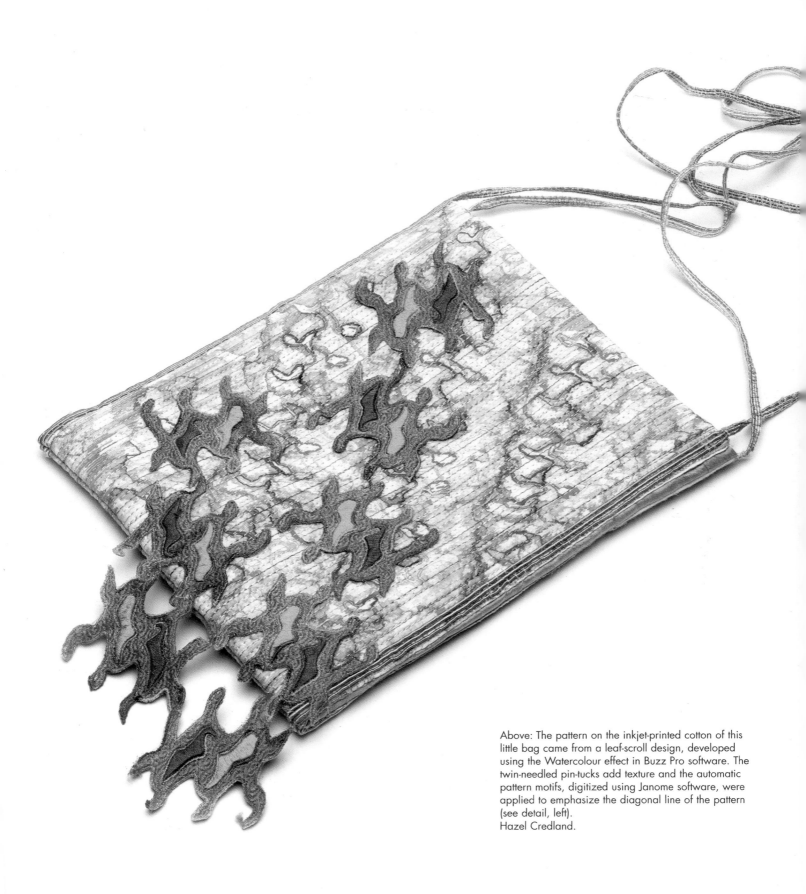

Above: The pattern on the inkjet-printed cotton of this little bag came from a leaf-scroll design, developed using the Watercolour effect in Buzz Pro software. The twin-needled pin-tucks add texture and the automatic pattern motifs, digitized using Janome software, were applied to emphasize the diagonal line of the pattern (see detail, left).
Hazel Credland.

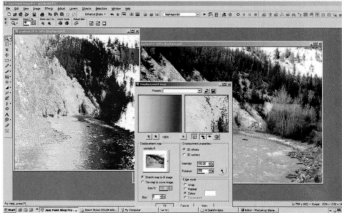

Above: A new page in a paint program was filled with bright colours and then an image of a lake and trees was used as a Displacement Map. This forced the colours to migrate into the shape of the landscape, as shown.

Left: This drawing of a cliffscape (detail shown) was produced using Graphitint pencils, and was wetted after use. It was scanned into a paint program and a photograph of the same landscape was used as a Displacement Map, changing the contours and subtly altering the look.

Displacement Maps

I love using the Displacement Map effect to make landscape studies. Here's how it's done:

1. In a paint program, paint some colours over the screen or fill with a suitable gradient colour. It could be wild primaries for a dramatically colourful effect, or go natural with autumn or summer schemes. Alternatively, use one of the 'swoopy' photos for colour. Let's call this image 1. Now open a digital photograph of a landscape, preferably one with lots of contrast like the one shown opposite.

2. Click on the coloured image (image 1) and then use the landscape pic for the displacement map. Most programs allow you to use any file open on the desktop as a map, so look for your landscape. Click OK and you should find that the colours have been forced into the shape of the landscape. Experiment with different images instead of image 1.

3. Print out on cotton or silk.

You could machine or hand stitch the image. Then print out words on sheer fabric and build up the embroidery with words in torn strips.

Right: *Long Beach*
50 x 20 cm (20 x 8 in)
The design was printed on cotton and stitched by hand and machine. The beach at the bottom was stitched with rows of running stitch to give the effect of sandy furrows.

Working a series

The scanner and software can be very useful for suggesting ideas for extending one piece of embroidery into a series. Scan in the completed textile or take a photograph of it. You'll then have the image to play with. Try cutting out areas and moving them or use one of the built-in Displacement Maps to change the image. The new image can then be printed onto print-ready fabric. You should be able to see some of the original stitching, which makes for an interesting base for further embellishment.

Above and right: The small embroidery by Valerie Campbell-Harding, right, was made by bonding and stitching strips of fabric, some muted and some bright, to a background. The shape was then free-machined over the top. The embroidery was then scanned into a paint program and used with a Displacement Map. This moved the design elements in interesting ways, as shown above.

Above: The new piece was inspired by a gauntlet seen in a museum. The displaced design, opposite, was constructed using prints on silk and ExtravOrganza. These were applied to felt as a base and Wireform was used to give a shape to the artefact. The edges were burned to resemble the distressed look of the original.

Sheer fabrics

Sheer fabrics have so many uses and printer-friendly sheets of organza (ExtravOrganza) and voile are now readily obtainable (see Useful Stuff, page 126). Consider the following:

- Print a design on both silk and organza. Place the silk on a stabilizer and hand or machine stitch. Lay the organza over the stitched silk and use an Embellisher machine to add gathers and texture.
- Lay a printed sheer over a stitched background to add shadowy images, or use it to provide a focal point for a painted background.
- Shadow quilting takes on a new dimension when a design is painted on a cotton background and overlaid with the same design in a sheer.

Try printing the same design on both cotton and sheer and mounting them, with a space between, putting the sheer fabric on top. This changes the image when it is viewed from different angles and is especially effective when the bottom layer is stitched, too. Work like this:

1. Print out a suitable image on cotton and sheer fabric.
2. Stitch the cotton layer (back it with felt or firm cotton) and stretch it over a strong card.
3. Now take a narrow strip of polystyrene, a lightweight wood baton or similar and cover it in toning fabric.
4. Glue it to the top of the cotton design, as shown in the diagram.
5. Cover the strip with PVA glue and stretch the sheer voile (unstitched) over it. Clamp it with bulldog clips until the glue dries, covering the fabric with baking paper to avoid marking.

This looks good mounted in a deep frame.

Another interesting way of using the sheer fabrics is to use two different images or to lay the sheer fabric over paper. This could be printed with the same image or one in which the size had been changed.

Covered strip glued over background

Above: Diagram showing one way of 'floating' a sheer fabric print over a solid one.

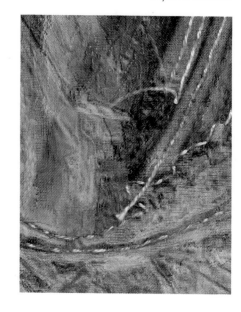

Below: Detail of piece shown on page 2. Glynda Morrison.

Opposite: *To Warm the Cockles of Your Heart.*
This textile piece is based around themes of family and reflects the fact that Siân's mother, Iris Martin, produced textiles based on the local cockle pickers of Penclawdd, Wales. A digital print of one of the women, printed on sheer fabric, is used on the manipulated fabric and the cockleshells. The title came from a favourite family saying.
Siân Martin.

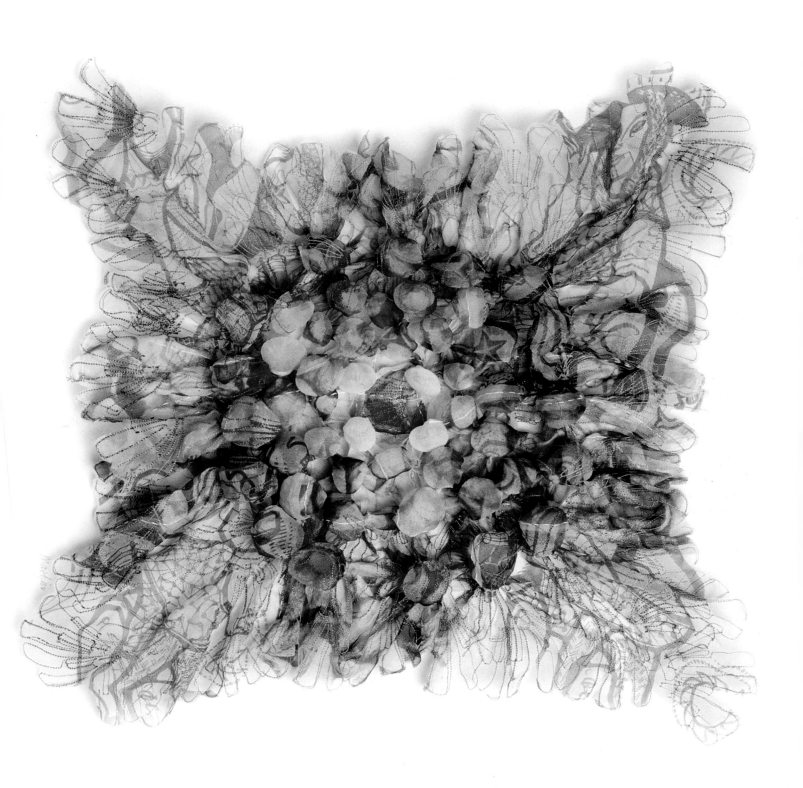

Paint techniques

A good way of making the most of print-ready materials is to print
some of the exciting designs created on paper that don't usually transfer
well to fabric. Everyday media, such as pencils, inks, paints and oilbars,
can be combined with techniques such as stamping, tracing and
monoprinting to produce exciting design ideas that can be transferred
to fabric. Enhance by adding some stitching, by hand or machine, to
produce stunning textiles. Here are three paint techniques to start you
off. I'm sure lots more ideas will come to you.

Method 1 Clingfilm

You have probably tried the fun technique of using clingfilm (also
known as Saran Wrap) over wet paint. This results in a wonderfully
colourful surface with an intricate tracing of lines. It's rather a busy
surface so it is best enlarged on the computer. Here is the method for a
clingfilm print:

1. Choose a firm paper that doesn't have an absorbent finish. Cartridge
   paper will do, and most commercial papers are fine. It shouldn't be
   too flimsy.
2. Paint or spray it lightly with water to help the paint spread. Then use
   a paint dropper or spray to apply three colours of ink, strong
   watercolour or spray paint. Add a little gold ink if you like.
3. Tear off some clingfilm, scrunch it up a little and lay it over the wet

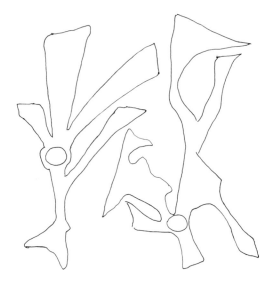

Above: Outlines of the shapes that were used
in the project.

Above: A clingfilm print was scanned and enlarged before it was printed on cotton fabric. It was textured with vertical lines of machine stitch. Shapes were traced (see opposite page) and cut out of painted fabric with seeding stitch used for texture. These shapes were applied to the background.

Below: Enlarged area of the clingfilm print showing the shapes that were traced. This is ready to be printed on transfer paper.

paint. Use your finger to move the paint about but don't mix the colour too much. Allow it plenty of time to dry and then remove the film.

You should have an exciting image with lots of crumpled lines. This is great but it is a little busy for using as a textile. To simplify it:

- Take it to your photocopy shop and ask them to blow it up to A3 (42 × 30cm, 16½ × 11¾ inches). Then, using two L-shaped pieces of card, choose an area from that and scan it into the computer.
- Alternatively, scan it into your computer using a 350dpi resolution. This will give you a big image. Use the Magnify tool to blow it up to full size (it will say 100%) and then use the Select tool to choose an interesting area. Save the file.

Print onto cotton fabric.

Stitching

Before stitching this fabric, make a tracing of some of the shapes thrown up by the enlarging process. You can see on the previous page the ones I have used.

The background will need some stitching and, if you want to texture it without obscuring the printed design, try this method.

Use the sewing machine to stitch straight lines over the image. Just set up the machine for normal sewing and use a stitch length of about 2. It is up to you whether or not the lines are spaced at regular intervals. I find that a thread colour that is slightly darker than the image gives a good result. When the background is complete, work on the tracings to produce raised shapes to use on top. Work like this:

1. Transfer your shapes from the tracing paper to Bondaweb (fusible webbing). You should be able to see the tracing through the webbing and you can draw on the paper side of the webbing with a pencil.
2. Paint some silk or cotton fabric with silk paints or use a suitable commercial material and iron the webbing onto the reverse.
3. Cut out the shapes and iron them onto heavy interfacing, such as craft Vilene.
4. Hand or machine stitch inside the shapes as desired and then cut them out.
5. Couch a yarn or metallic thread around the edges of each shape and apply to the background, moving the shapes around to find the position that looks good.
6. Finally, decide how to finish the edges. They could be trimmed and mounted as a rectangular shape or cut out with a soldering iron.

Opposite: Detail of stitched shapes on printed background showing seeding stitch and wrapped cords.

Method 2 Sgraffito

This method involves placing colour over a background, usually with wax crayons or oil pastels, and then using a sharp tool to remove some of the colour. Try this:

1. Use a black background or paint black paint on firm paper and allow it to dry completely.
2. Now cover the paper in blocks of colour from wax crayons or Markal (Shiva) oilbars – my favourite for this technique.
3. Then use a sharp point – a large needle, the point of a craft knife or a serrated knife – to scratch out lines and reveal the background. (You can buy special tools but they are not really necessary.)
4. Consider stitch marks when doing the scratching. This technique is great for designing for hand stitching.

It is also possible to work this technique by using coloured pencils and then painting with black poster paint, before scratching back. This works but is not as good as the Markal.

Work as described for the clingfilm design to make an interesting surface for hand or machine stitching.

Left: This design made use of sgraffito techniques by working on black paper and building up layers of Markal (Shiva) Oilbars. This top layer was scratched back to reveal the lower surface.
Valerie Campbell-Harding.

Opposite: The detail shows an enlarged area suitable for stitching.

Method 3 Monoprints

An interesting design exercise, encountered at a workshop led by Ruth Issett, involved half of the class (wearing colourful garments and trailing floaty scarves) moving in dance-like poses while the rest of the class made lightning sketches. There was then a swap, so that everyone produced a mini portfolio of shape and colour studies, concentrating on movement.

We then used screen-printing inks (but acrylics work well) to ink up a glass plate and drew into it, following the colours and shapes of our initial sketches. Pressing paper onto the glass picked up the paint.

The basic lines of the monoprint were fleshed out by enhancing some areas with Markal (Shiva) oilbars and finally a wash of Procion dye was painted over. This gives a great effect when used with the oilbars.

Finally, these paintings were cut up and collaged onto a new background and everyone in the group produced an embroidery from the design. It would be a great way to theme a group exhibition, as there were common elements from the design source but many different techniques were used.

These designs could be scanned, printed and stitched, as before.

Above: The design shown right was scanned into the computer and printed on cotton, reversing one of the images. Hand and machine stitching techniques were used to build up the textile before it was machined to Wireform and shaped.

Opposite: a design that evolved from a study of figurative movement. The shapes were interpreted using mono-printing techniques, Markal (Shiva) Oilbars and Procion dyes.

Bubble Jet Set 2000

It is possible to make your own fabric into a printable surface. Bubble Jet
Set 2000 works very well with regard to light- and wash-fastness but I find
that the results are not as sharp as the commercially prepared fabrics. It is
certainly much cheaper and can be a very useful means of making a
washable, lightfast cloth with a soft handle. It is fine for backgrounds where
the crispness of the image is not an issue. Bubble Jet Set 2000 can also be
useful in cases where you want to try out a technique before using a more
expensive print-ready fabric, so it's great for experiments. I like to use it for
lightweight silk with an Embellisher (needle-felting) machine.

The finer the fabric, the better the result – closely woven firm fabrics
work best. The ink in your printer can make a big difference with Bubble
Jet Set 2000, and could be a reason why your friend gets good results and
you don't. See Appendix 2 for ways to improve the print quality when
using this product. To use the product:

1. Cut the fabric to size for your printer.
2. Soak it for 5 minutes in the solution and then allow it to dry.
3. Iron it onto freezer paper to carry it through the printer.
4. Print, using a high-quality print setting and glossy paper as the paper type.
5. Leave for 30 minutes before washing with detergent and lots of water.
   The makers recommend a washing machine but I use a kitchen sink for
   small pieces. Don't fold them and don't heat-set before washing.

Above: A supplier's inspiration pack, containing
a variety of yarns and fabrics, was scanned into
a paint program. A displacement map (a
drawing of an ammonite) was used to produce
a design that was printed on fine silk. This was
applied to felt with an Embellisher machine and
the surface was enhanced with silk fibres and
ribbon. The lack of detail in the Bubble Jet Set
2000 print does not matter here as it is distorted
by the machine. A detail is shown below.

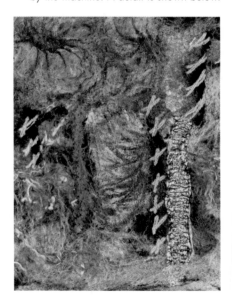

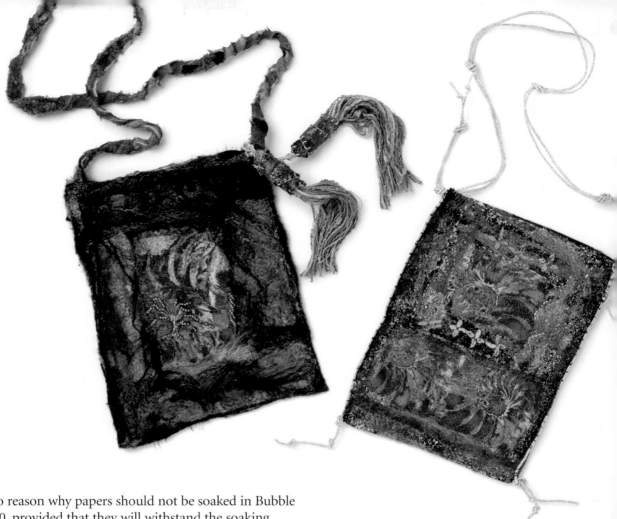

There is no reason why papers should not be soaked in Bubble Jet Set 2000, provided that they will withstand the soaking process. I have found that even tissue paper can be used if it is laid onto a non-stick sheet and then has the solution sprayed onto it. Alternatively, bond the tissue to a surface with Bondaweb (fusible webbing) and then soak the whole piece. This gives the paper a much improved lightfast quality.

If you like to use Bubble Jet Set 2000, I'd suggest that you soak the fabric in good-sized lengths so that you don't have to wait for each piece to dry.

Above: Bags made using the embellished silk design. Silk fibres, velvet ribbon and black chiffon were used with an Embellisher machine. The printed fabric was applied and the result was hand stitched. This stitching was attacked by the Embellisher to sink it into the fabric. The bags were made by Embellishing the sides to join them.

Left: These samples show the difference between Bubble Jet Set 2000 and a ready-to-print fabric. This does not matter if the fabric is to be Embellished or heavily stitched.

Blueprint (Cyanotype) fabric

This process uses ready-prepared fabric that has been impregnated with light-reactive chemicals. It will be sent to you in a lightproof pack so don't open it until you are ready to use it, and then do any cutting in a darkened room. You can make your own fabric – but that is for another book (there's lots of information on the web). The process works brilliantly with a computer-printed transparency. Here's how:

1. Make your design, which should have a black-and-white colour scheme with lots of contrast. Try using an image from one of the Search Press books (see page 127).
2. Turn the image to a negative image.
3. Print it on an inkjet transparency.
4. Lay it flat on the fabric and expose it to the light. You will need a reasonably sunny day, although it will work in hazy sunlight. Exposure can be anything from 4 minutes in the summer to 15 minutes in winter sun, so do a test run first on a small piece. The longer it is left, the darker it will become and the design will show far less.
5. When exposure is completed, rinse the print in clean, cold water until it runs clear and dry away from direct light.

Print-ready fabrics are so immediate. They are there ready when inspiration strikes. They have a soft handle and can be used for garments – provided they are pieced together. For me, the most exciting part is their role in transferring paper artwork. I've always wanted to stitch into a clingfilm design and now, thanks to these fabrics, I can.

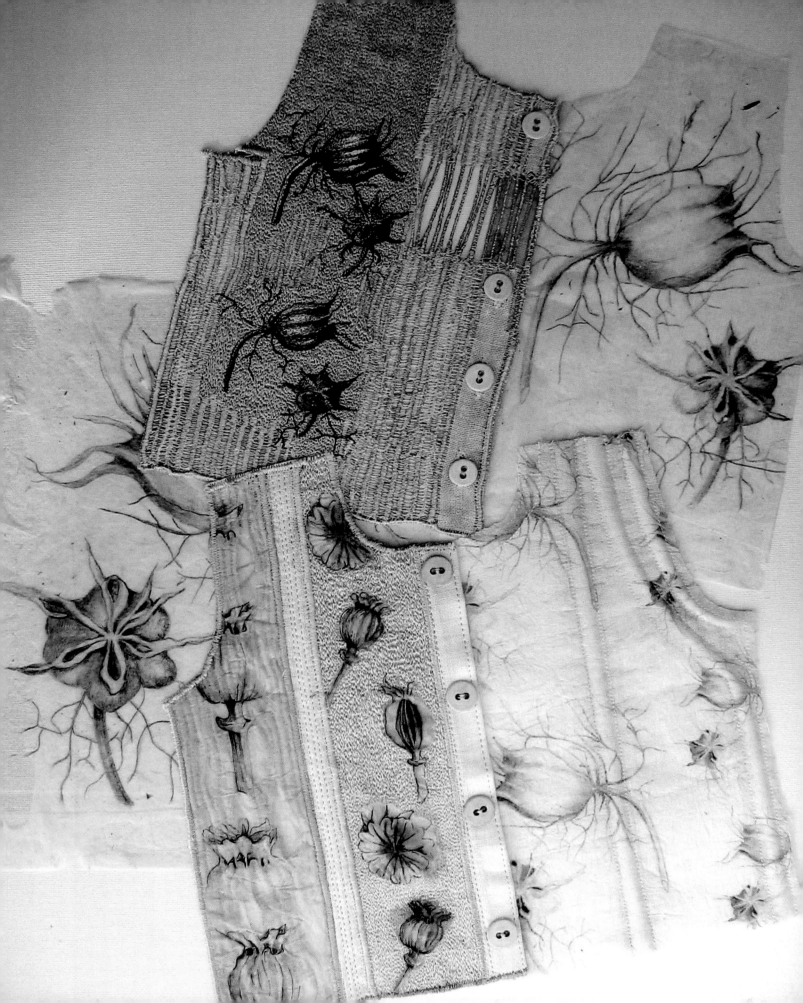

Iron-over transfer paper

Inkjet iron-over transfer paper is a very accessible and useful paper for design transfer. Easily purchased from stationers, computer stores and even supermarkets, it may also be called T-shirt transfer paper.

It can be used in a similar manner to the printable fabrics we have been looking at but there are advantages in the fact that it is first printed and then ironed onto a surface. This gives infinite possibilities for stitching or manipulating the surface before ironing the print over. The printed paper can also be changed by cutting, tearing, scrubbing and scraping. This gives wonderful opportunities for creating textiles with an aged appearance. The paper produces fabric that is washable and lightfast but it may feel a little stiff or have a plastic-like coating, and is not usually suitable for wearable art where a drape is needed.

Opposite: *Whirlwind.*
A transfer print was ironed onto cotton and the central motif was heavily stitched with free running stitch. The stitching is not so dense on the background areas of the image.
Margaret Talbot.

Right: Packs of transfer paper, which are often sold as T-shirt transfer paper.

Using transfer paper

You will probably find when purchasing the paper that there are various brands on offer: some well-known names, some own brands, cool-peel, hot-peel, dark and light fabrics, and so on. Most of them work very well, although the very cheap ones can have a rather plastic finish. As with so much else, you get what you pay for.

If you are using a dark fabric background, you will need the specific paper for this, although I find it a little obvious and it doesn't integrate as well as the light-on-light. Try a couple of different brands using the same image and record the result.

Most transfer paper will reverse the image. An exception to this is the paper sold by Crafty Computer Paper; with this paper the image is melted into the fabric from the top and is not reversed. An important point to remember then, when printing on the majority of papers, is to reverse the print, as it will appear as a mirror image when ironed to fabric. This may not matter with an abstract or photographic design but is vital with lettering. Look at your printer controls and select the 'Mirror Image' facility, which will automatically reverse the print. See Appendix 2, page 124, on printing.

It is also important to read the information sheet in the paper pack so that you print on the correct side of the sheet. Most of the papers have text or graphics on the reverse of the paper; some have a clipped corner. Adjust the printer controls to a high-quality image, as before, so that you get the best possible print.

Opposite: *A Stitch in Time*
16.5 x 15.5 cm (6½ x 6 inches)
A heat-transferred digital print was ironed onto cotton and dupion silk. The techniques used were reverse appliqué with running stitch in lines as dictated by the design.
Olga Norris.

Right: This effect was obtained by scanning the reverse of a stitched design of a face and figure (Leonardo Da Vinci's Vitruvian Man). The result was enhanced in a paint program with lettering and added motifs. This was then printed on cotton and free machine stitching was added to produce these two small pieces.
Carla Mines.

When you have printed your sheet, you must again consult the instructions as the different makes of paper vary a little in the ironing time and heat. As a general rule, the fabric onto which you are ironing the print should be placed on a thin piece of fabric over a hard, heat-proof surface and ironed for several minutes with a hot iron. Don't use a steam setting (keep the iron moving slightly to avoid marks from the steam holes.)

Some of the papers are 'cool-peel' and these you leave for a while before peeling off the paper. Others can be peeled straight away. If there is any suggestion of 'shininess' after the paper is removed, simply iron again, placing non-stick baking paper between the iron and the printed fabric to protect both the iron and your design.

With regard to fabrics, cotton or polycotton (with a good percentage of cotton) work well. Later in this section we look at some other fabrics. I find that silk doesn't work at all well, as it is often left with a shiny, rather greasy look.

Above and below: A transfer-print motif (above) was cut out and ironed to a background of painted fabric. Further areas were cut out before it was heavily machine and hand stitched, and formed into a decorative bag.

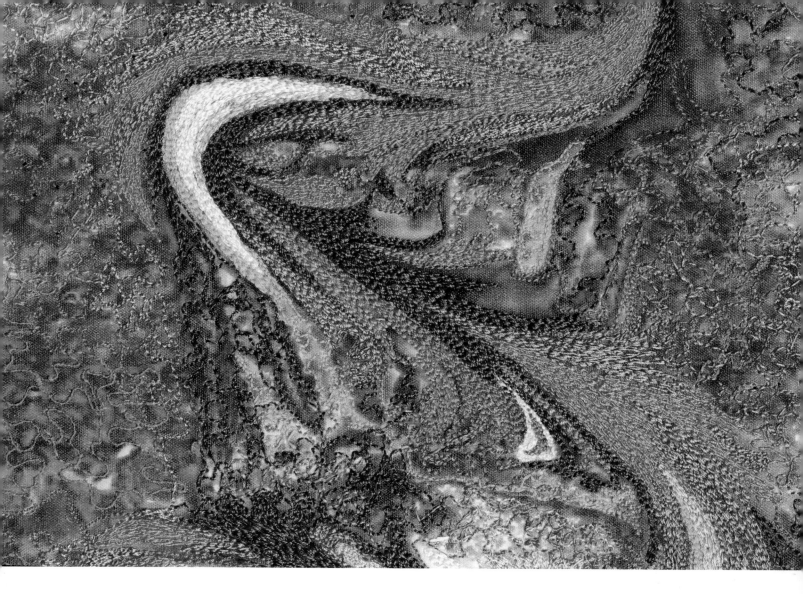

Here are some basic ideas for fabric and stitch:

- Iron the print onto a sturdy fabric such as cotton. Use a stabilizer or place the printed cotton on another piece of cotton fabric or felt and use a temporary adhesive to hold the fabrics while you stitch. Then free-machine over the print, following the areas of the design. Don't machine heavily – leave some parts of it free. Use free running stitch on the main areas and then add a little whip stitch for accents. Some hand stitching will add a dimensional element. Try adding it first and then machining into it.

Above: Detail of *Whirlwind* (the whole of which can be seen on page 88), showing how the background printing can be seen through stitch while the main motif is heavily embroidered. Margaret Talbot.

- Try using pale velvet instead of cotton. Put it on a strong background fabric and spray with a temporary adhesive to hold the fabrics together – velvet is a slippery customer if it is not stabilized. Spray the top surface lightly with a temporary adhesive and then place some wisps of silk or nylon fibres (tops) onto the velvet before ironing over the print. Stitch a little into the design using free running stitch and following the flowing lines of the silk. Work some motifs on water-soluble fabric, remembering to overlock the stitches, or work a grid first. Place the water-soluble motifs on the background and either stitch them into it or leave them as 'floating' elements.
- Stamp with Xpandaprint or a similar puff paint after ironing the print onto cotton. While it is still wet, sprinkle embossing powder over it and heat with a heat tool. Don't print all over the fabric; leave some room for stitching. Free-machine in the spaces between the puff paint to complete the work.
- Cut out a motif or single element and iron it onto a previously painted or dyed background.

Below: A digital photograph of plants in pots was transfer-printed onto cotton. Some scrim was stitched on and areas were highlighted with machine embroidery. Puff paint in a dark colour was stamped over the top of this to give texture. Treasure Gold wax was then rubbed over to highlight the raised areas.

Cut and slash

Here's an idea for an interesting twist, using cutting and slashing techniques.

1. Take a digital photograph, perhaps a floral theme. Print on transfer paper and transfer to cotton.
2. Use one of the special effects in your imaging program to change the image substantially, for instance a Displacement Map or a Swirl filter. Intensify the colour too, by using an Inked Edges filter. Print onto black cotton using a transfer paper for dark fabric.
3. Lay the second (dark) piece over the first, right sides together, and stitch a 2.5cm (1in) square grid.
4. Cut into the top fabric, cutting across every other square, as shown in the diagram. Take care to cut into just the top fabric, not through both thicknesses.
5. Fold the edges to meet in the centre of the next square.

The advantage of using transfer paper is that the cut edges will not fray. The dark fabric makes a good contrast and is more interesting as it shows on the top of the work. An alternative would be to use a light fabric on top but give it a pale colour wash to take away the stark whiteness.

Above: 'Cut and slash' stitched piece made into a small folded book. The designs used were Gaudi-inspired, architectural images. The top fabric uses transfer paper for dark colours. Wrapped washers and cords add texture and detail.

Below: Diagram showing where to cut in a 'cut and slash' design.

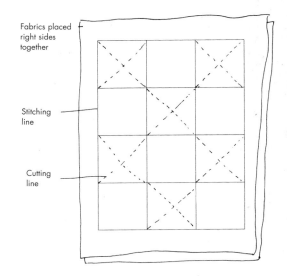

Fabrics placed right sides together

Stitching line

Cutting line

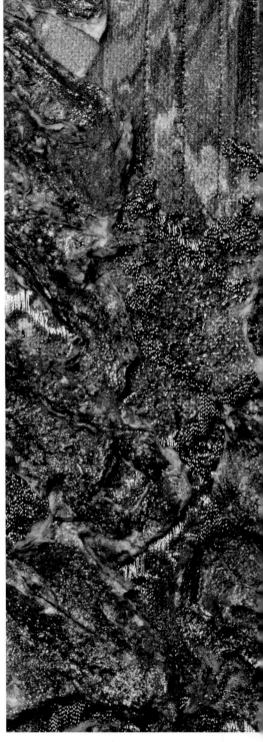

Soldered surfaces

The soldering iron can be used in many ways to add texture and interest to a transfer print. Here are two methods.

Method 1 Tissue on Vilene

1. Iron a transfer print onto cotton and add lines of stitch or spot patterns.
2. Now iron crumpled tissue paper onto pelmet (craft) Vilene.
3. Paint this tissue/Vilene fabric in a colour that contrasts or tones with the stitched transfer print.
4. Use a hot soldering iron to burn and cut away areas of the tissued Vilene and re-apply over the print with additional stitching by hand or machine.

Method 2 Soldered Lutradur

Lutradur is a 'geotextile' used in industry but easily available. Printing directly onto Lutradur makes for a very pale print but ironing a transfer print onto it gives a more accurate result. It works well with a soldering iron.

It is possible to use these differences to advantage by making a direct print as a background and then producing another print with a transfer image. You will then have one pale fabric and one with deeper tones. The transfer print should be related to the background but with clear motifs, or defined areas, to cut out.

Work like this:

1. Print directly on the Lutradur, mounting it first on a carrier paper.
2. Print the related image on transfer paper.
3. Iron the transfer paper onto the Lutradur and peel off. Iron again under baking paper if it is too shiny.
4. Place the pale Lutradur onto a stabilizer (felt or cotton) and do a little background stitching. Stitch in straight lines or follow the patterns. Don't make this stitching too obvious.
5. Use the soldering iron on the transferred image. It should have much more defined colour and detail. Cut out the shapes carefully; see if you can also use the negative shapes that are left after cutting out.
6. Apply the cut-outs using stab stitches to keep them free from the background.

Right: The background to this piece is a transfer-printed design. On top of this is a printed tissue paper on a Vilene structure, which has been soldered to provide additional texture and reveal the background.

Opposite, top: Printed Lutradur was used as a background for this piece with a design source based on bubbles. The same design was printed on transfer paper and ironed onto heavier Lutradur. This gives a much clearer image. Some areas were then carved out with a soldering iron and applied on top of the print. Small crystal beads were added to enhance the watery effect.
Ann Goodwin.

Opposite, bottom: the same method was used for this piece but the background design was achieved using a special effect in a paint program, the result of which was printed directly onto Lutradur. This was stitched with a pattern of random lines. The transfer print with the motif was ironed onto Lutradur as before and the motifs were then soldered out and applied with beads to build up the surface.
Susan Hughes.

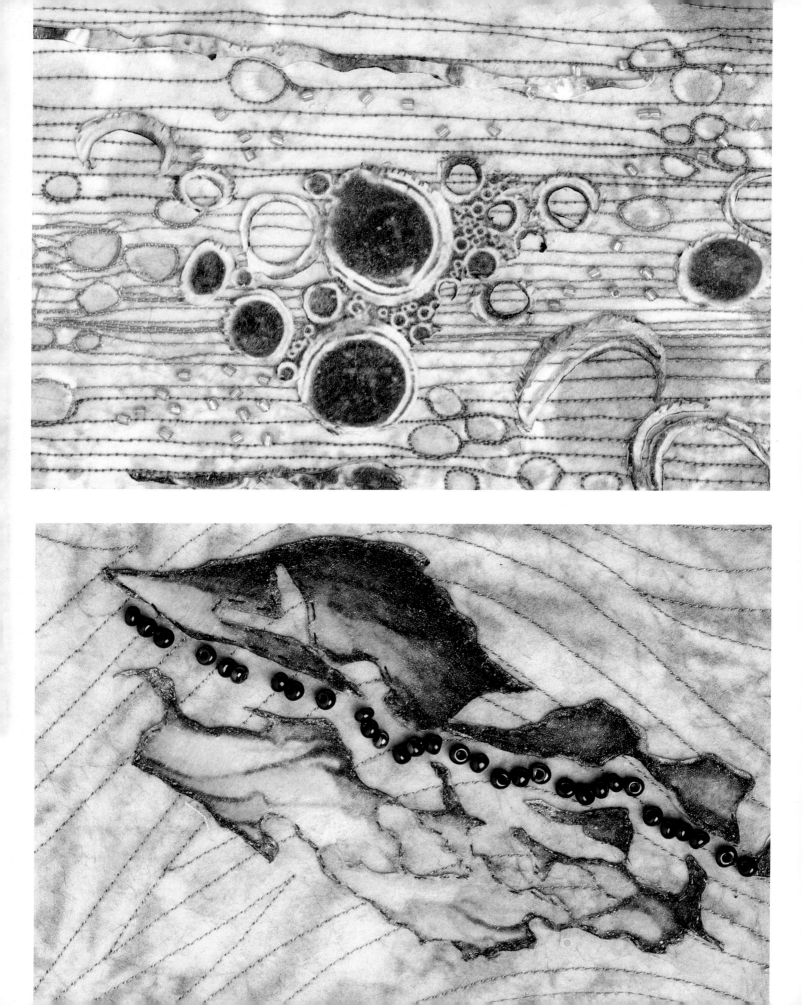

Ironing onto texture

Preparing a surface

So far, we have only touched lightly on ways to prepare a surface. The great advantage of ironing the print onto the fabric is that it is possible to build up the surface on which you will be ironing. In Section 1, we looked at printing on brown or tissue paper and then crumpling it. With transfer paper, you could iron a print straight onto a crumpled surface like this, which would give a very interesting effect.

Carry this forward and consider ironing onto lace, pintucks, stitching or even a surface that has been heavily textured with an Embellisher machine. How about transferring to a surface that has previously been decorated with a print block and gold paint?

Think about resists – laying a cut shape on the surface and ironing over the top. The transfer will be prevented from colouring the resisted area. Tearing up the transfer paper would work well, too.

Not all transfer papers are suitable for ironing over textures as some are too dense. I have had good results from the Hewlett Packard and Hyatt brand (sold in the UK as Jet FX). If you want a considerable amount of the surface to show, try rubbing at the print with a wire pot-scourer or sandpaper. This will allow far more of the textured surface to show through. If you do this, consider using creamy-coloured fabrics as white can be very stark.

Above: In this piece, based on a Dorset landscape, the transfer print was torn before ironing onto a base fabric textured with lace and scrim. This was then enhanced using an Embellisher machine with fibres and threads. Betty Ruffell.

Opposite: This delightful garden print was made by ironing a transfer print onto a background that had been built up with scraps of lace, scrim and other textural fabrics. Jenny Younger.

Ironing onto lace

Stitch some lace (not too chunky – something like net-curtain weight) onto a piece of cotton that has been lightly sprayed with dilute walnut ink or tea-dyed. Iron the transfer paper over the top. There will be areas where the transfer has missed and that is the reason for colouring the cotton – white is often too great a contrast. If you use a heavier lace, it may even be that the print will only transfer onto the lace and not the background. This could leave you with a lacy pattern on the transfer paper to iron onto another piece of fabric.

Ironing onto appliqué can also give good results. Apply shapes in a variety of white or pale fabrics onto cotton and iron over.

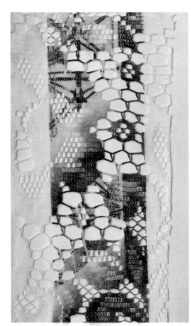

Above: Torn lace was treated with a transfer print as before, with the loose areas pulled away and placed on the top.

Right: Sample of transfer print ironed over lace.

Opposite: Here we can see a detail of an embroidery made by first bonding lace to a cotton base. Then some machine stitching was added before the transfer print was ironed on top.
Maureen Beale.

Ironing onto stitching

Try ironing over a stitched surface. Use a background with a high percentage of cotton and stitch with pale thread to blend, or metallic to add glitz.

Try stitching:
- straight lines
- lines of zigzag
- pintucks
- couched threads or yarns
- heavy areas of cable stitch with other 'quiet' areas not stitched.

Don't forget about using the scourer technique to remove some of the surface of the print. Try to avoid a stark white surface and work on creamy coloured fabrics. Iron in the usual way.

As with the lace, you may find that some of the techniques – the pintucks for instance – leave part of the design on the paper, enabling you to use the paper again.

Ironing onto tearable or zappable fabrics

Think about ironing a transfer onto more unusual materials. Sheers, muslins and scrims can be torn up and placed on the surface. Chiffon, acrylic felt or metallic organza can be zapped with a heat tool to produce fragments. You don't need to stitch first.

- Experiment with small pieces, layering up a mix of all these fabrics onto baking paper before ironing over.
- Iron the transfer print really well and don't try to do a big piece. Small works well.
- If you have chiffons or organzas, use the heat tool after transferring the print.

If the result is shiny due to the heat tool, paint it with matt acrylic varnish after stitching.

Opposite: *Turkey in Sepia*
Digital photographs were combined with tea-dyed raised embroidery. The heavily stitched surface was built up in 'tiles' and faggoting techniques were used to join the pieces.
Margaret Talbot.

Above left: Stitched surface with some of the print rubbed away before ironing over.

Above right: Here, the surface was built up with stitch over soft applied fabrics before the transfer print was ironed over. Some of the loose pieces were then torn and reapplied over the top.

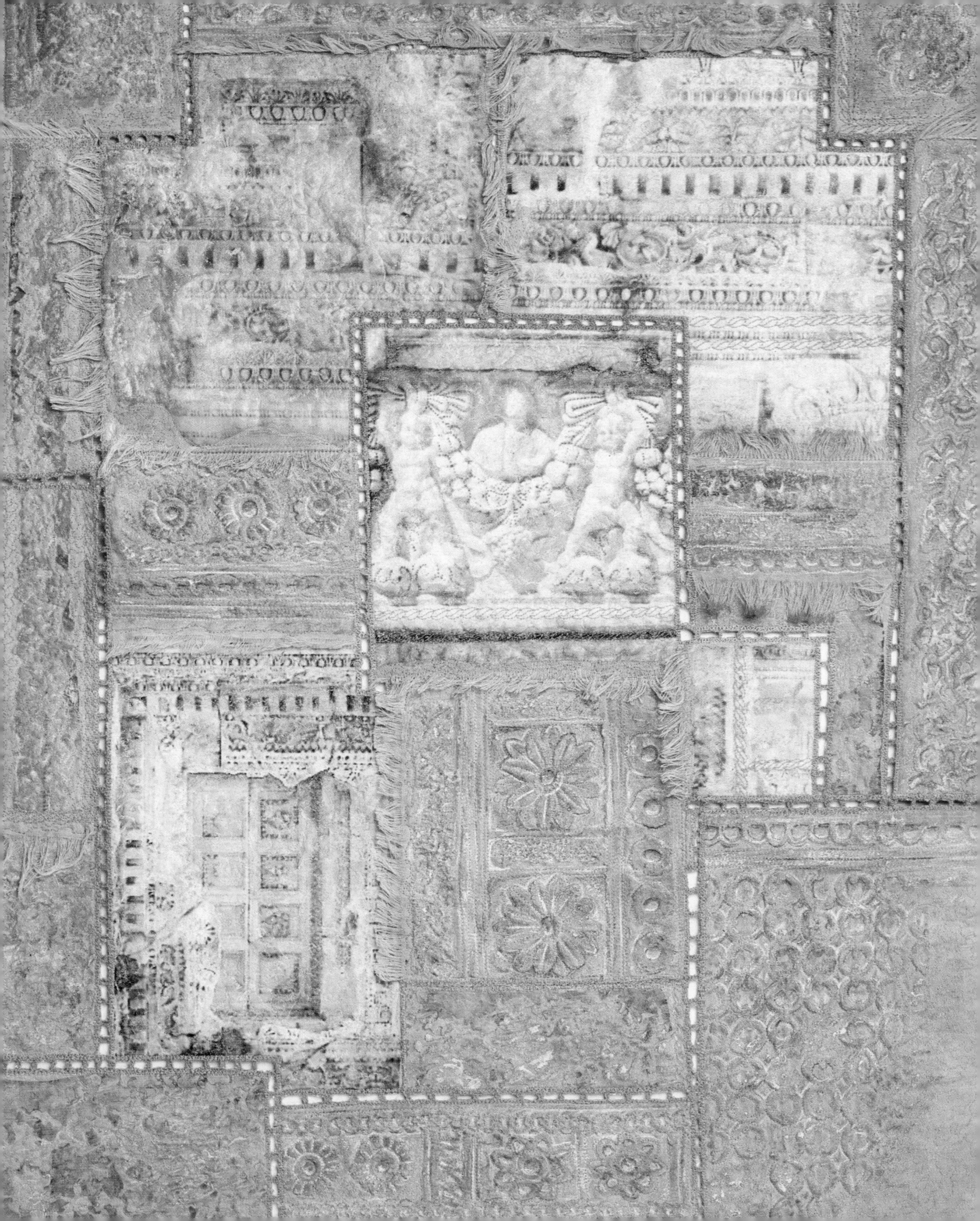

Further ideas for transfers

So far we've looked at different ways to build a surface to produce exciting embroideries. Here are some more intricate ideas.

Dissolvable film

An interesting effect can be created by stitching in white thread on water-soluble film, adding snippets of scrim and lace. Build up a design with contrasts of fabric. Stitch and leave lots of space. Dissolve and dry and then iron a transfer print onto the piece. Transfer the same design onto cotton and then stitch the dissolvable film over the cotton print.

Crumpled baked silk

This makes a really interesting surface:

1. Stitch fine habutai silk with gold thread – either lines of pattern or random areas of free machining.
2. Dampen the fabric and scrunch it up in your hand.
3. Place it (still scrunched) in an old metal baking dish in a hot oven for about 20 minutes. Watch it carefully – it should turn a lovely golden brown but not be burnt.
4. Let it get cold and then iron Bondaweb (fusible webbing) onto felt. Place the silk on top, pulling it out but not flattening it. Iron through baking paper.
5. Iron a transfer print onto the crumpled silk surface.

Tissue paper, bonded to fabric, also makes an interesting surface. As before, consider the base colour and try not to use a stark white paper; spray with dilute walnut ink or weak tea.

Opposite: *Cambridge Blue*
A scrunched and crumpled tissue paper background was used as a base for the print that originated from a digital photograph. This was then bonded onto tea-dyed felt and gilded.
Margaret Talbot.

Below: Crumpled baked silk overlaid with skeleton leaves. A transfer print of the monoprint image from page 82 was ironed over the top.

Preparing surfaces for an Embellisher machine

An Embellisher (needle felting) machine can be used to great effect with inkjet transfers. It means that textures can quickly be built up and it enables unusual fabrics to be held to a background. I like to work by laying down texture, ironing over the transfer and then building up more fibres on top. The scouring technique (attacking the transfer paper with sandpaper) is particularly useful here, as more background can be shown.

Consider the following:

- Embellish light-coloured yarns to the background.
- Build up surfaces in colours that complement the print you are using. Rub out some of the transfer print to show the colours below.
- Embellish squares using different fabric textures. Rub out a little of the print, as before.
- Use knobbly silk noils, gummed silk waste and similar for a heavily textured ground fabric. Add scrim and iron well; this will flatten it a little. After ironing, use the point of a pair of scissors to lift the fibres.

Another really exciting result from an Embellisher machine can be obtained by ironing a transfer onto coloured felt and working from the back to bring colour and texture into the work. As the transfer paper often stiffens the fabric, this approach is less likely to break needles. Lay other fabrics on the back (dark muslin is great) and work on those to push subtle colour through. This technique is great for shading.

Above: An Embellisher machine was used to build up a surface using silk noil and scrim with pale felt as a background. A scoured print was ironed over this.

Opposite: A landscape transfer print was ironed onto acrylic felt that had been textured with neutral-coloured fibres using an Embellisher machine. This was then treated with a heat tool on the back of the work in order to buckle it.

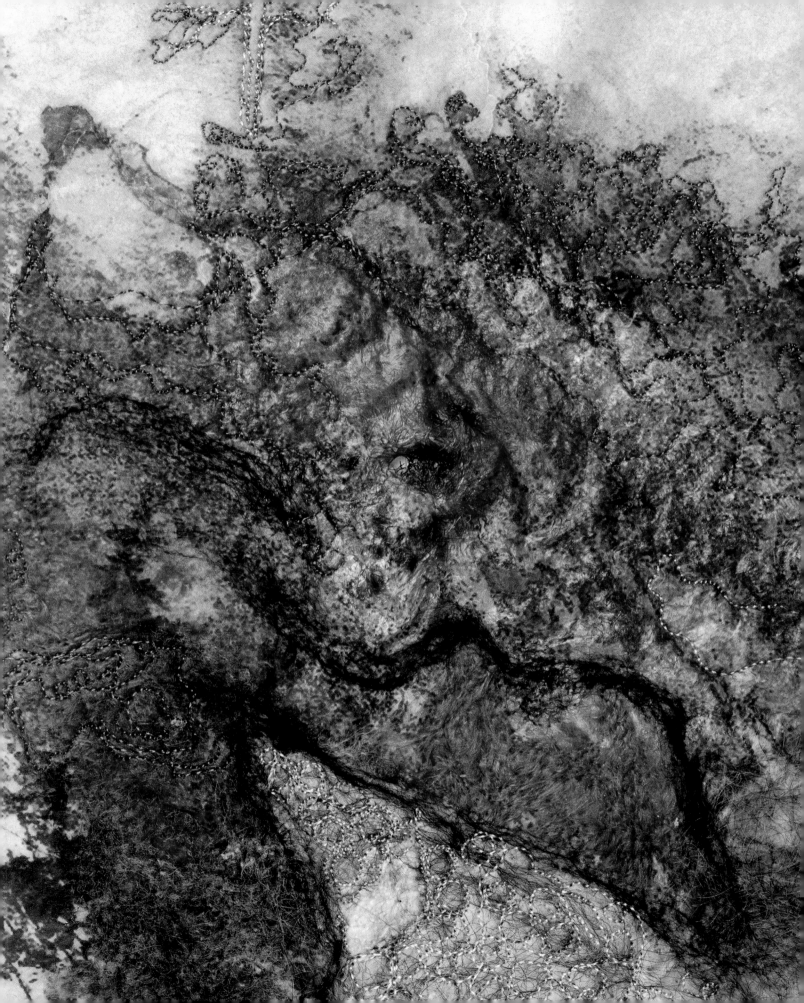

Distressed effects

We have been scratching out areas of the image before ironing it in order to show more of the surface. This technique can be extended to other designs, such as those that represent old wall paintings, manuscripts or icons. Try these effects before ironing:

- Use a knife to scrape heavy areas in a linear fashion.
- Crease or fold the transfer paper and use the knife along the lines.
- Rub with sandpaper to remove lots of surface. Use an image with lettering (remember to reverse the print) as a base for manuscript studies. It can also be fun to leave the lettering and allow it to reverse.

If you would like a lot of the background to show through the scrapings, you might consider colouring the fabric lightly, as a stark white area can stand out too much. Well diluted tea or coffee will give a pale wash and dilute walnut ink is an ideal background as it has good colourfast qualities. Try some samples to get the colour right. When you are happy, paint on the colour or dip the fabric into a container containing tea or coffee. Allow to dry thoroughly before ironing over the transfer print.

An ideal background for a textile based on old text or a faded wall painting is crumpled tissue paper. To give this a good base, prepare it as follows:

- Iron Bondaweb (fusible webbing) to felt or Vilene and then iron the tissue paper onto it.
- Now iron the scraped image onto the crumpled tissue.
- Stitch tea-dyed agricultural fleece or nappy (diaper) liner over the top in some places, using an automatic pattern.
- Catch the top lightly with a gold Markal (Shiva) stick.
- Use a heat tool to distress the fleece. (You can see examples of this technique on page 110.)

Above: Two more pieces that show the effect of scraping or scratching before ironing the print to show more of the surface. One of these has been printed with a stamp before ironing.

Opposite: This photograph, taken in an old chapel, was printed on transfer paper and ironed onto cotton over a pin-tucked, stamped surface. The same print was ironed onto Lutradur and the figures burned out with a soldering iron before being applied to the background surface.

Below: Scraping the paper before ironing onto the background gives this machine-embroidered work the look of an old fresco.

There is so much that can be done with inkjet transfer paper and, once you start experimenting, lots more ideas will come. Always try a small piece before leaping in with a whole sheet.

Printing on fabric with an inkjet printer provides a range of possibilities, from the ready-to-print fabric, which gives an immediate surface for stitch, to the more complex surfaces built up and coloured with transfer paper.

Below: In these samples, text-printed transfers were ironed onto walnut ink-painted tissue bonded to Vilene. Before ironing, the prints were scrubbed with a pan scourer to give the effect of an ancient manuscript. Agricultural fleece was dyed with tea and stitched on top. The prints were then distressed with a heat tool. In both cases, Ultra Thick Embossing Enamel was then melted on the surface and a stamp pressed into it. They will form a base for further stitching.

Summary of techniques

Product	For	Against	Best For
Ready Print Fabrics (pre-treated)	Quick and easy. Good, sharp print. Lightfast. Washable with care. Soft handle.	Expensive. Limited choice of fabric.	Fine for all applications. Sheers are very useful and provide interesting effects when layered.
Bubble Jet Set 2000	Inexpensive way of making pre-treated fabric. Soft handle. Use any fabric.	Less sharp images. Time-consuming. Fades more quickly.	Experiments. Textiles that will be quite heavily stitched. Using with an Embellisher machine. Using innovative fabrics.
Cyanotype fabric	Good effects from transparencies.	Needs sunshine. Needs care with fabric storage.	Trying a range of effects with different images. Good for matching with indigo-dyed fabrics.
Iron-over (T-shirt) transfer paper	Not too expensive. Easy to find. Can be ironed onto a variety of surfaces. Doesn't fray.	Waxy feel. Stiff handle to fabric. Expensive for experiments. Can be rubbed away.	Ironing on top of textures – stitch or embellishment. Rub-away effect is great for distressed effects or to show the background.

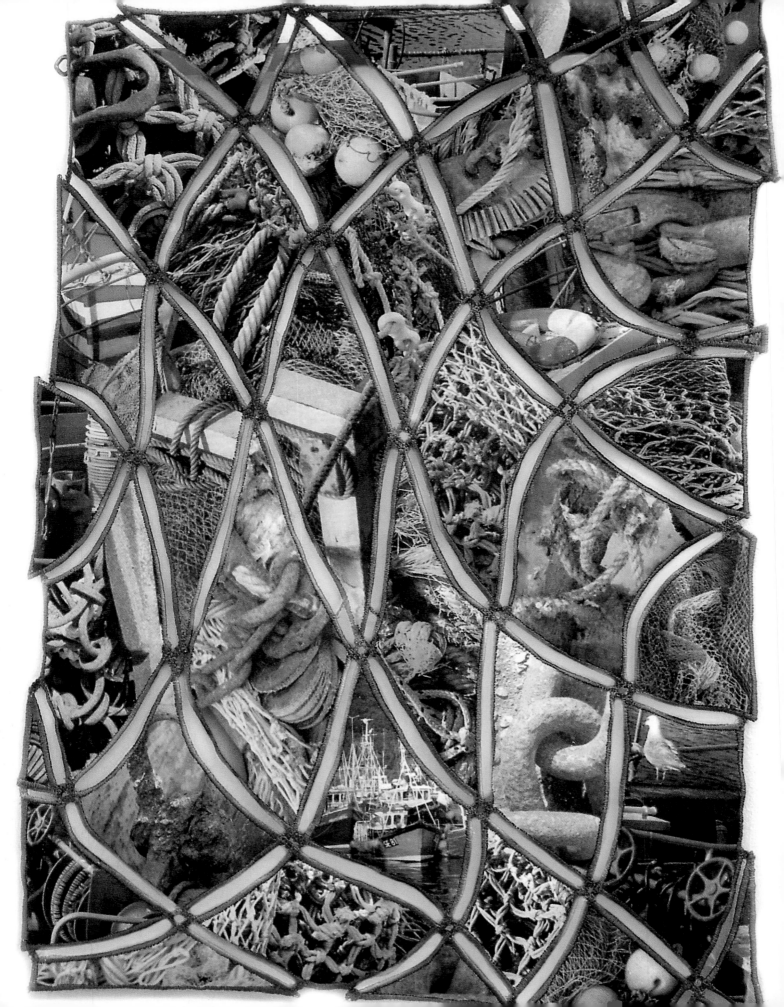

Conclusion

I can't end the book without looking at the ways in which the different methods we have been examining can be extended and combined. The use of different materials can provide a contrast which, if carefully considered, can enhance the work. It is also essential to move beyond the single-page capabilities of the basic inkjet printer, and the methods of constructing larger pieces are considered here.

Large-scale work

Large embroideries can be produced by purchasing print-ready fabric by the metre. This can then be taken to one of the specialized printers that undertake this work. It is generally printed on an A3 (42 × 30 cm, 16½ × 11¾ inch) printer and is usually quite reasonably priced, considering the size involved. Larger than A3 does get more expensive. Back the fabrics by ironing onto stabilizer or use batting if the work is to be quilted.

Many of the printing establishments have their own fabric but it is also possible to buy your own and have the design printed on it. You can see from the work shown here how effective these large pieces can be.

Previous page: *Ullapool Quay.* Holiday photographs were printed using transfer paper. They were then faggotted together in the manner of a fishing net. Margaret Talbot.

Left: A really good way to build up large designs is shown here. The design elements are all based on flint patterns on the walls of East Anglian churches. This lends itself to this approach, in which small units (in this case, transfer prints ironed onto polycotton) are faggotted together to make a book cover. Margaret Talbot.

Opposite and below: *Solarised Tulip.* The fabric for this large tulip piece was printed onto cotton by a specialist printer. Hand stitches were used to enhance areas of the design (see right), which was produced using the Solarize filter in Photoshop Elements. Carol Dowsett.

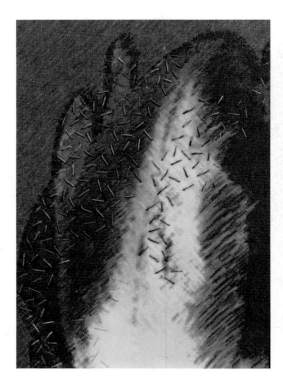

Putting it all together: where to go from here

Don't be afraid to mix up the transfer methods and use several together, as long as they fit in with the work. It can help to provide a contrast as the surfaces are likely to be different. It's also easier to make larger pieces with some methods than others.

Photo collages

Try using photographs to make collages. Print out the photos on good paper to achieve a crisp print – an interesting twist could be to enlarge some areas. Cut up the prints and stick them onto a background. You could:

- Overlap the cut-outs.
- Colour some areas with pencil, pastel or marker.
- Paste the cut-outs on long, thin or curved backgrounds.

The results can be used as a design guide to the finished piece or could be scanned and printed onto fabric, ready for stitching. If it is a long piece, scan in sections and make a feature of the overlap. Alternatively, consider photocopying to a larger size and using a rub-away method.

Above: This piece, *Schism*, is based on Adam and Eve and their expulsion from Eden. The design (shown below) was built up by cutting up photographs to make a wide collage. It was transferred by using the 'Picture This' rub-off method for the main area, with scrolls made from stitched silk prints on paper at each end.

Below: *Schism* design.

Piecing

Joining the transferred fabrics need not just mean piecing them as a quilt. Think about a long thin strip combining pieces of varying height, or a long thin strip with wrapped cords or other embellishments dangling from it.

Use Wireform to give joined pieces a rippled effect, or work a large three-dimensional structure such as the one shown here, based on an Italian church on a clifftop. It was translated into a tower structure using heavy Vilene.

This was worked by:

1. Painting the heavy Vilene with acrylic paint to form the sky.
2. Printing the scene onto transfer paper and ironing this onto a normal-weight Vilene.
3. Cutting out the church shape with a soldering iron and using PVA glue to fix it to the painted background.

Further cotton prints were machine embroidered to add interest to the base, and two further towers were made to form an installation.

Top: *Towers* 60 x 50 cm (24 x 20 inches)
These large, free-standing structures were made from heavy craft Vilene which was painted as a background. The scenes were printed on cotton and bonded to a normal-weight Vilene, which was glued to the heavier tower shape after stitching. Smaller embroideries cluster at the base.

Above: The diagram shows possibilities for joining pieces together.

Another option for making large-scale work would be to cut up the fabrics and join them to form a larger work. This could be contrived using standard patchwork techniques. I am not a patchworker so my preferred method is to take a large piece of felt and place the stitched pieces of printed fabric onto it, holding them with temporary adhesive before stitching. I leave room between them for a form of sashing. For me, this is usually painted or printed paper bonded to dark felt. With this pinned in place, I stitch straight lines across the sashing to secure it, over the pieces, to the background.

The work shown here is based on a Moorish prayer shirt, worn for devotions. It occurred to me that today's equivalent to those devotions would be shopping. So the shirt was based on scenes from catwalk shows, shopping malls and so on, all transferred to fabric. Dissolved water-soluble paper drapes over the shirt, representing the erosion of the old religion.

I hope you feel inspired by these techniques and that you will consider them a starting point for your own work. New materials are being discovered all the time, so keep watching the Internet. Do continue to record, print, stitch and generally experiment with all manner of images and media.

Above: Some areas of the water-soluble paper were dabbed with puff paint and gilded.

Below left: One of the images used for the piece opposite. It was reversed before being printed onto transfer paper.

Below right: The top layer represents the old religion being eroded by the new. Water-soluble paper was stitched with lines before some were washed away.

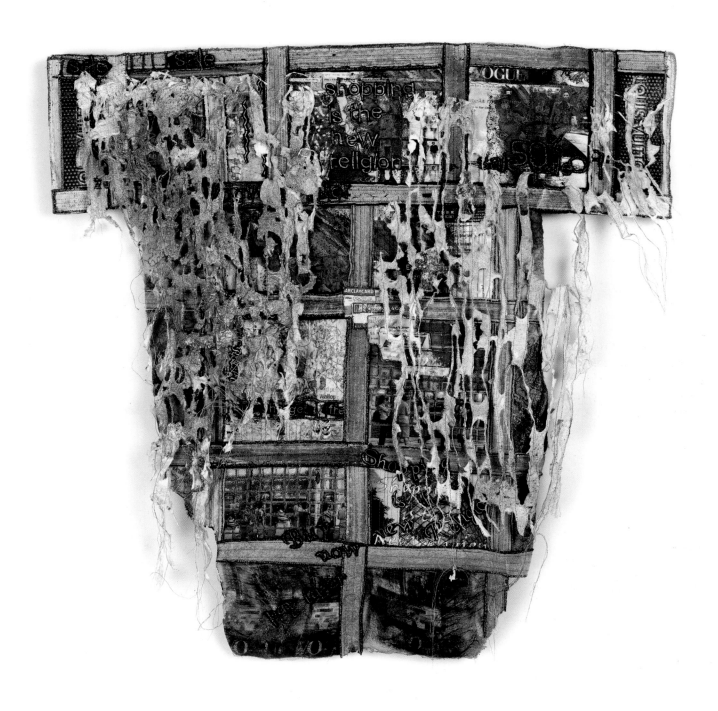

Above: *Shopping is the New Religion*
90 x 60 cm (36 x 24 inches)
Based on a prayer shirt, this textile explores the idea
of religion past (the tattered overlay) being eroded by
the new religion of designer wear and shopping. It
uses transfer-printer paper with stitch and surfaces
eroded using an Embellisher machine.

Appendix 1
Cameras and Scanners

Digital cameras

Digital cameras can be useful in capturing subjects that are difficult to scan or that are in areas of low light. For holiday memories or close-ups of texture, they extend the design options and give us a wonderful range of images to work on. Having made the purchase, there is no processing cost whatever, apart from printing out your images. Make sure that you buy a camera with a reasonably high megapixel level. It should have a good lens – this makes so much difference. A macro button is essential as you will find it invaluable for close-ups. You may or may not need a high-factor zoom option (they need a good stabilization system or a tripod) but base your decision only on the optical, not the digital, zoom. Invest in a 'What Camera'-type magazine – it's worth the cost. Once the images have been captured with the digital camera, transfer them to the computer using the card reader, plugging in the camera to a USB connection or using a wi-fi link.

Left: Screen shot of a one-step photo menu.

Hints and tips on digital cameras

Many of these ideas were passed on to me by my friend Valerie Campbell-Harding, sadly no longer with us.

1 Avoiding the shakes

If you cannot use a tripod or a bean bag, try to lean against something that is solid, such as a wall or a tree, or even another person. You could also bend down and lean your elbows on your knees to steady yourself.

Look at your screen to check on the shutter speed. It should not be less than 1/125 sec – faster if you are using the zoom.

2 Composition

Most pictures have too much detail in them, so try to avoid the cluttered background. Walk around to find another viewpoint, or get in closer to the subject. Simplicity is often the key, especially for using the photograph as the base for a computer design.

When you have taken a photo, think for a moment about whether you could have taken a better one. Try another side, or the back. Bend down, kneel or lie on the ground and point the camera upwards. Or stand up and point the camera downwards. Different viewpoints can make all the difference between an ordinary photograph and a stunning one.

3 Light

Get used to your EV (Exposure Value) button to change the amount of light coming through the lens. The camera will always measure very darks and very lights as a mid grey, so if there are a lot of light areas in your picture, let more light in by adjusting your EV to 'plus'. If there are a lot of dark areas in your picture, then adjust the EV to 'minus'.

For fun, adjust the colour temperature. For example, if you are taking a photograph in daylight, look in your menu to find the setting for fluorescent or incandescent lighting, and see what happens. Different cameras have different settings and yours might be called 'cloudy', or 'indoors', or 'night'. Try them all. You can see the results on the screen so you can press the shutter, or not, as you wish.

4 Getting in close

Most digital cameras allow you to get in much closer than would be the case with compact cameras. However, to make the best use of this feature, you must use the screen to compose the photograph, not the viewfinder.

Getting in close is often the key to getting an interesting, but simple, composition, and certainly cuts out the clutter that ruins most photographs. This will help your design later on. Getting in close shows you interesting patterns and textures – and lovely shapes – that you might otherwise miss when using a longer viewpoint. Try it and see.

Think about using a digital camera to build up a texture library of patterns. This is an excellent idea and can be a trip down memory lane when you access it.

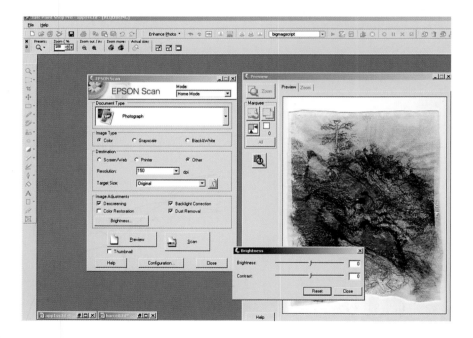

Left: Screen shot of scanner software.

Scanning

Scanners sold these days are usually A4-sized flatbeds (30 x 21 cm, 11¾ x 8¼ inches), often combined with printers. They can be used with their own software or from within most paint or image programs. Look for the Import command in the File menu. Scanners are very easy to use but don't forget the snag – a high resolution A4 image in full colour can take up a huge amount of memory and disk space. Although less important now that most machines come with a lot of memory and hard disk space, storing huge images has a lot of drawbacks. Having said that, it's important not to go too low or you will not get a good print.

For scanning, the factor that influences the size of an image as stored is the resolution, generally expressed as dots per inch (dpi). The higher the resolution, the more the dots and the more storage space is needed. I usually use 150 dpi. Look at the box that opens when you select the scan option. This will allow you to change the resolution settings. It will often have different options, such as illustration or photograph. Choose the most suitable. Don't be afraid to try some of the settings in your Image Adjustment menu. Some, such as the Brightness control, can be very useful. The box that you see when you open the software depends on the manufacturer, but a typical one is shown below left.

Images can be stored in a number of different formats. If you store images as .jpg, they will degrade every time you save them because of the compression factor. So, if you are going to do a lot of work on an image, save it as a .tif file.

What to scan? Anything and everything, as long as it is not too sticky! Be careful with 'debris' such as skeleton leaves, which may lose bits under the scanner lid. Trap them between acetate sheets to be safe. Try scanning with the lid up, moving the item down or along as you scan.

As discussed in the book, I like to scan my completed embroideries on full colour, then take areas and play with them. This can extend a single embroidery into a series, often in ways you wouldn't expect – a real bonus. Think about scanning to add texture. Tree barks, snake skins or even heat-buckled paper give spectacular results as backgrounds when used as described in the earlier chapters. Try three-dimensional objects – some interesting diversions can happen.

The Computer Textile Design Group (www.ctdg.co.uk) has produced an excellent booklet called 'Scanners, Scanning, Scans' which is well worth working through.

Copyright

A word of warning on scanners and digital cameras: bear in mind the copyright laws and only scan your own or copyright-free material. Always ask before you take photographs – even if it is a colourful market stall.

Appendix 2
Printing your Images

This book is not the place to go into great depth about colour matching or aligning screen and printer. Most image processing programs have colour optimizers that do a pretty good balancing act to give you a good print. This is probably all you need but it is important to find out how to access the Printer Properties menu. In most cases this just involves:

1. Going to the Print menu, clicking Print and then selecting the box marked Properties.
2. From the resulting menu, choose the Best Photo option and the paper type, based on the paper that you intend to use.
3. Clicking on the Page Layout button gives options such as mirror printing, number of copies and so on.
4. Find the button to allow a print preview, which prevents nasty surprises such as a postage-stamp-size image.

If you are unhappy with the printed result you could try to enhance the image in the software. Options such as Clarify and Sharpen may help, but be aware that it is easy to overdo these – particularly the Sharpen command. If in doubt, always view the image at 100% and look at the edge for signs of 'halos'. Sharpen the pic and look closely, then undo and look again. Choose the best option.

If all else fails, explore your printer driver's Advanced option. You may have an SRGB (Standard Red Green Blue colour space) button, which can make a big difference to the print.

Remember above all that you are not trying for photographer of the year and that you will be using the print as a base for stitching. For general photographs, it is often worth sending the files to a specialist agency – they do a great job and it may even be cheaper than printing out all your holiday photographs on the inkjet.

Print layouts

Some programs have a Print Layout command under the File menu. This will show all the files you have open in a side window and you can drag them onto the page. Here, they can be resized, rotated and generally made to fit the page. Several pics can be shown and this is a great option for getting the most out of a page that is to be photocopied or where special fabric will be printed.

The screenshot below shows a page prepared for printing. The images overlap the edge of the paper to use every bit of it.

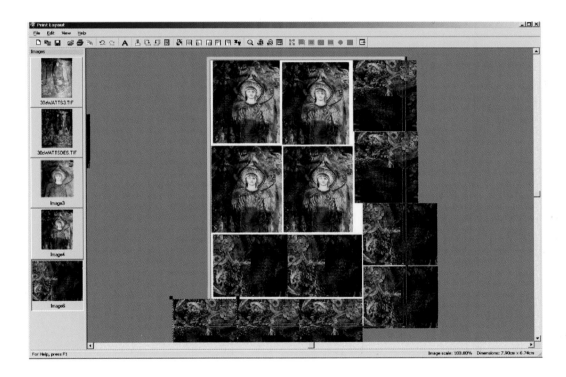

Left: Screen shot of a print layout window from the Paint Shop Pro program.

Useful Stuff

Suppliers

UK

Ario
5 Pengry Road
Loughor
Swansea
SA4 6PH
fiona@ario.co.uk
www.ario.co.uk
Art supplies, Bubble Jet Set 2000,
Jacquard printable fabrics (cotton, silk,
organza), Lutradur, Markal (Shiva),
Moon Shadow Mists, Paper Perfect,
Picture This, Procion dyes, Tissutex,
Transfoil, Wireform, Xpandaprint,
505 spray

Art Van Go
The Studios
1 Stevenage Road
Knebworth
Hertfordshire
SG3 6AN
art@artvango.co.uk
www.artvango.co.uk
Art supplies, wide range of papers
including Japanese and Lokta,
Dimensional Paints, FuseFX, InkAID,
Jacquard printable fabrics, JetFX
(excellent transfer paper), Liquitex
Blended Fibres, Markal, Paper Perfect,
Picture This, Procion dyes, Tissutex,
Transfoil, Translucent Liquid Sculpey,
Wireform, Xpandaprint, 505 spray

Crafty Computer Paper
Woodhall
Barasford
Hexham
Northumberland
NE48 4DB
sales@craftycomputerpaper.co.uk
www.craftycomputerpaper.co.uk
All speciality papers, Dry Rub-Off
Decals, non-reverse transfer and
printable fabrics. Also website good
for giving information

Gillsew
Boundary House
Moor Common
Lane End
High Wycombe
Buckinghamshire
HP14 3HR
info@gillsew.co.uk
www.gillsew.co.uk
Transfer and direct print papers,
general supplies, Cyanotype fabric

Ivy House Studio
37 High Street
Kessingland
Suffolk
NR33 7QQ
ivyhousestudio@hotmail.com
www.ivyhousestudio.com
Craft Vilene, Image Maker, Jacquard
printable fabrics, Markal, Paper
Perfect, Procion dyes, Transfoil,
Wireform, Xpandaprint, 505 spray

Oliver Twists
22 Phoenix Road
Crowther
Washington
Tyne and Wear
NE38 0AD
jean@olivertwists.freeserve.co.uk
Inspiration packs, wide range of
threads and fibres, metal shim,
abaca tissue

Rainbow Silks
85 High Street
Great Missenden
Buckinghamshire
HP16 0AL
caroline@rainbowsilks.co.uk
www.rainbowsilks.co.uk
Alcohol inks, Bubble Jet Set 2000, Craft
Vilene, cyanotype fabric, distress inks,
embossing powder, Jacquard printable
fabrics, Lutradur, Markal, Paper
Perfect, Picture This, Procion dyes,
Tissutex, Transfoil, Translucent Liquid
Sculpey, Wireform, Xpandaprint,
505 spray

Whaleys (Bradford) Ltd
Harris Court
Great Horton
Bradford
West Yorkshire
BD7 4EQ
info@whaleysltd.co.uk
www.whaleys-bradford.ltd.uk
Inkjet fabric by the metre; most
other fabrics

Winifred Cottage
17 Elms Road
Fleet
Hampshire
GU51 3EG
sales@winifredcottage.co.uk
www.winifredcottage.co.uk
Craft Vilene, Lutradur, Tissutex,
505 spray, many other supplies

PC World, Staples, etc.
Various outlets nationwide
HP and Epson transfer paper

USA

American Art Clay
www.amaco.com
Art materials and metal

Impress Me Now
www.impressmenow.com
Rubber stamps

Meinke Toy
www.meinketoy.com
Most supplies

Quilting Arts
www.quiltingarts.com
Most supplies

CANADA

Stitches, Quilts and Yarns
www.stitchesquiltshop.com
Most supplies

AUSTRALIA

The Thread Studio
6 Smith Street
Perth
WA6000
Australia
mail@thethreadstudio.com
www.thethreadstudio.com
Most items

Software

Corel PaintShop Pro
Paint program

Photoshop Elements
Paint program
Try Amazon for both of these
(www.amazon.co.uk)

Picasa
www.picasa.google.com
Free photo management program

Websites

giving useful advice on materials
and general computing

Computer Textile Design Group
www.ctdg.co.uk
*Good books on design, scanning, and
other computer stuff*

InkAID
www.inkaid.com
Lots of information on their products

Quiltwow
www.quiltwow.com
*Internet magazine for quilters,
with good articles on using images*

Workshop on the Web
www.workshopontheweb.com
*Internet magazine for textile artists,
with good articles on using images*

Books and CDs

*Creating Sketchbooks for Embroiderers
and Textile Artists*
Kay Greenlees
Batsford, 2005
www.anovabooks.com

Paper, Metal and Stitch
Maggie Grey and Jane Wild
Batsford, 2004
www.anovabooks.com

A Sketch in Time
Jan Beaney and Jean Littlejohn
Double Trouble Enterprises, 2003
www.doubletrouble-ent.com

Dover Books
store.doverpublications.com
*Books and CDs with copyright-
free images*

Search Press
www.searchpress.com
*Books and CDs with copyright-
free images*

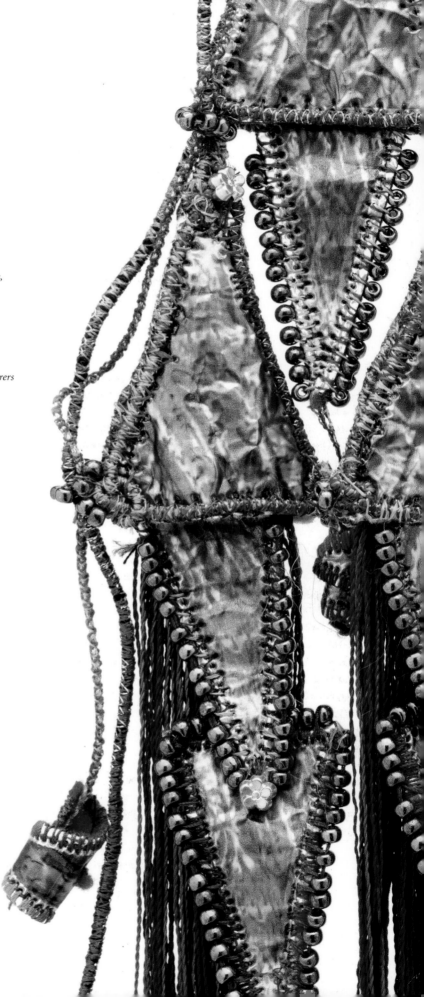

Index

Right: This box uses Dry Rub-Off Decals (see page 46) on both metal and wood. Hazel Credland.